The Attributes of God:
The Essence of the Divine

John Calvin; Caleb Sinclair

GRAPEVINE INDIA

Published by

GRAPEVINE INDIA PUBLISHERS PVT LTD

www.grapevineindia.com
Delhi | Mumbai
email: grapevineindiapublishers@gmail.com

Ordering Information:
Quantity sales: Special discounts are available on quantity
purchases by corporations, associations, and others.
For details, reach out to the publisher.

First published by Grapevine India 2023

Welcome to our Christian book collection!

For access to more Christian audiobooks,

send a blank email to

thegoodchristian10@gmail.com.

.

Contents

1.

The Nature and Tendency of the Knowledge of God.

By the knowledge of God, I intend not merely a notion that there is such a Being, but also an acquaintance with whatever we ought to know concerning Him, conducing to his glory and our benefit. For we cannot with propriety say, there is any knowledge of God where there is no religion or piety. I have no reference here to that species of knowledge by which men, lost and condemned in themselves, apprehend God the Redeemer in Christ the Mediator; but only to that first and simple knowledge, to which the genuine order of nature would lead us, if Adam had retained his innocence. For though, in the present ruined state of human nature, no man will ever perceive God to be a Father, or the Author of salvation, or in any respect propitious, but as pacified by the mediation of Christ; yet it is one thing to understand, that God our Maker supports us by his power, governs us by his providence, nourishes us by his goodness, and follows us with blessings of every kind, and another to embrace the grace of reconciliation proposed to us in Christ. Therefore, since God is first manifested, both in the structure of the world and in the general tenor of Scripture, simply as the Creator, and afterwards reveals himself in the person of Christ as a Redeemer, hence arises a twofold knowledge of him; of which the former is first to be considered, and the other will follow in its proper place. For though our mind cannot conceive of God, without ascribing some worship to him, it will not be sufficient merely to apprehend that he is the only proper object of universal worship and adoration, unless we are also persuaded that he is the fountain of all good, and seek for none but in him. This I maintain, not only because he sustains the universe, as he once made it, by his infinite power, governs it by his wisdom, preserves it by his goodness, and especially reigns over the human race in righteousness and judgment, exercising a merciful forbearance, and defending them by his protection; but because there cannot be found the least particle of wisdom, light, righteousness, power, rectitude, or sincere truth which does not proceed from him, and claim him for its author: we should therefore learn to expect and supplicate all these things from him, and thankfully to acknowledge what he gives us. For this sense of the divine perfections is calculated to teach us piety, which produces religion. By piety, I mean a reverence and love of God, arising from a knowledge of his benefits. For, till men are sensible that they owe every thing to God, that they are supported by his paternal care, that he is the Author of all the blessings they enjoy, and that nothing should be sought independently of him, they will never voluntarily submit to his authority; they will never truly and cordially devote themselves to his service, unless they rely upon him alone for true felicity.

II. Cold and frivolous, then, are the speculations of those who employ themselves in disquisitions on the essence of God, when it would be more interesting to us to become acquainted with his character, and to know what is agreeable to his nature. For what end is answered by professing, with Epicurus, that there is a God, who, discarding all concern about the world, indulges himself in perpetual inactivity? What benefit arises from the knowledge of a God with whom we have no concern? Our knowledge of God should rather tend, first, to teach us fear and reverence; and, secondly, to instruct us to implore all good at his hand, and to render him the praise of all that we receive. For how can you entertain a thought of God without immediately reflecting, that, being a creature of his formation, you must, by right of creation, be subject to his authority? that you are indebted to him for your life, and that all your actions should be done with reference to him? If this be true, it certainly follows that your life is miserably corrupt, unless it be regulated by a desire of obeying him, since his will ought to be the rule of our conduct. Nor can you have a clear view of him without discovering him to be the fountain and origin of all good. This would produce a desire of union to him, and confidence in him, if the human mind were not seduced by its own depravity from the right path of investigation. For, even at the first, the pious mind dreams not of any imaginary deity, but contemplates only the one true God; and, concerning him, indulges not the fictions of fancy, but, content with believing him to be such as he reveals himself, uses the most diligent and unremitting caution, lest it should fall into error by a rash and presumptuous transgression of his will. He who thus knows him, sensible that all things are subject to his control, confides in him as his Guardian and Protector, and unreservedly commits himself to his care. Assured that he is the author of all blessings, in distress or want he immediately flies to his protection, and expects his aid. Persuaded of his goodness and mercy, he relies on him with unlimited confidence, nor doubts of finding in his clemency a remedy provided for all his evils. Knowing him to be his Lord and Father, he concludes that he ought to mark his government in all things, revere his majesty, endeavour to promote his glory, and obey his commands. Perceiving him to be a just Judge, armed with severity for the punishment of crimes, he keeps his tribunal always in view, and is restrained by fear from provoking his wrath. Yet he is not so terrified at the apprehension of his justice, as to wish to evade it, even if escape were possible; but loves him as much in punishing the wicked as in blessing the pious, because he believes it as necessary to his glory to punish the impious and abandoned, as to reward the righteous with eternal life. Besides, he restrains himself from sin, not merely from a dread of vengeance, but because he loves and reveres God as his Father, honours and worships him as his Lord, and, even though there were no hell, would shudder at the thought of offending him. See, then, the nature of pure and genuine religion. It consists in faith, united with a serious fear of God, comprehending a voluntary reverence, and producing legitimate worship agreeable to the injunctions of the law. And this requires to be the more carefully remarked, because men in general render to God a formal worship, but very few truly reverence him; while great ostentation in ceremonies is universally displayed, but sincerity of heart is rarely to be found.

2.

All Idolatrous Worship Discountenanced in The Scripture, by Its Exclusive Opposition of the True God to All the Fictitious Deities of the Heathen.

But, since we have shown that the knowledge of God, which is otherwise exhibited without obscurity in the structure of the world, and in all the creatures, is yet more familiarly and clearly unfolded in the word, it will be useful to examine, whether the representation, which the Lord gives us of himself in the Scripture, agrees with the portraiture which he had before been pleased to delineate in his works. This is indeed an extensive subject, if we intended to dwell on a particular discussion of it. But I shall content myself with suggesting some hints, by which the minds of the pious may learn what ought to be their principal objects of investigation in Scripture concerning God, and may be directed to a certain end in that inquiry. I do not yet allude to the peculiar covenant which distinguished the descendants of Abraham from the rest of the nations. For in receiving, by gratuitous adoption, those who were his enemies into the number of his children, God even then manifested himself as a Redeemer; but we are still treating of that knowledge which relates to the creation of the world, without ascending to Christ the Mediator. But though it will be useful soon to cite some passages from the New Testament, (since that also demonstrates the power of God in the creation, and his providence in the conservation of the world,) yet I wish the reader to be apprized of the point now intended to be discussed, that he may not pass the limits which the subject prescribes. At present, then, let it suffice to understand how God, the former of heaven and earth, governs the world which he hath made. Both his paternal goodness, and the beneficent inclinations of his will, are every where celebrated; and examples are given of his severity, which discover him to be the righteous punisher of iniquities, especially where his forbearance produces no salutary effects upon the obstinate.

II. In some places, indeed, we are favoured with more explicit descriptions, which exhibit to our view an exact representation of his genuine countenance. For Moses, in the description which he gives of it, certainly appears to have intended a brief comprehension of all that it was possible for men to know concerning him—"The Lord, the Lord God, merciful and gracious, long suffering, and abundant in goodness and truth, keeping mercy for thousands, forgiving iniquity, and transgression, and sin, and that will by no means clear the guilty; visiting the iniquity of the fathers upon the children, and upon the children's children." Where we may observe, first, the assertion of his eternity and self-existence, in that magnificent name, which is twice repeated; and secondly, the celebration of his attributes, giving us a description, not of what he is in himself, but of what he is to us, that our knowledge of him may consist rather in a lively perception, than in vain and airy speculation. Here we find an enumeration of the same perfections which, as we have remarked, are illustriously displayed both in heaven and on earth—clemency, goodness, mercy, justice, judgment, and truth. For power is comprised in the word Elohim, God. The prophets distinguish him by the same epithets, when they intend a complete exhibition of his holy name. But, to avoid the necessity of quoting many passages, let us content ourselves at present with referring to one Psalm; which contains such an accurate summary of all his perfections, that nothing seems to be omitted. And yet it contains nothing but what may be known from a contemplation of the creatures. Thus, by the teaching of experience, we perceive God to be just what he declares himself in his word. In Jeremiah, where he announces in what characters he will be known by us, he gives a description, not so full, but to the same effect—"Let him that glorieth glory in this, that he understandeth and knoweth me, that I am the Lord, which exercise loving-kindness, judgment, and righteousness in the earth." These three things it is certainly of the highest importance for us to know— mercy, in which alone consists all our salvation; judgment, which is executed on the wicked every day, and awaits them in a still heavier degree to eternal destruction; righteousness, by which the faithful are preserved, and most graciously supported. When you understand these things, the prophecy declares that you have abundant reason for glorying in God. Nor is this representation chargeable with an omission of his truth, or his power, or his holiness, or his goodness. For how could we have that knowledge, which is here required, of his righteousness, mercy, and judgment, unless it were supported by his inflexible veracity? And how could we believe that he governed the world in judgment and justice, if we were ignorant of his power? And whence proceeds his mercy, but from his goodness? If all his ways, then, are mercy, judgment, and righteousness, holiness also must be conspicuously displayed in them. Moreover, the knowledge of God, which is afforded us in the Scriptures, is designed for the same end as that which we derive from the creatures: it invites us first to the fear of God, and then to confidence in him; that we may learn to honour him with perfect innocence of life, and sincere obedience to his will, and to place all our dependence on his goodness.

III. But here I intend to comprise a summary of the general doctrine. And, first, let the reader observe, that the Scripture, in order to direct us to the true God, expressly excludes and rejects all the gods of the heathen; because, in almost all ages, religion has been generally corrupted. It is true, indeed, that the name of one supreme God has been universally known and celebrated. For those who used to worship a multitude of deities, whenever they spake according to the genuine sense of nature, used simply the name of God, in the singular number, as though they were contented with one God. And this was wisely remarked by Justin Martyr, who for this purpose wrote a book *On the Monarchy of God*, in which he demonstrates, from numerous testimonies, that the unity of God was a principle universally impressed on the hearts of men. Tertullian also proves the same point from the common phraseology. But since all men, without exception, have by their own vanity been drawn into erroneous notions, and so their understandings have become vain, all their natural perception of the Divine unity has only served to render them inexcusable. For even the wisest of them evidently betray the vagrant uncertainty of their minds, when they wish for some god to assist them, and in their vows call upon unknown and fabulous deities. Besides, in imagining the existence of many natures in God, though they did not entertain such absurd notions as the ignorant vulgar concerning Jupiter, Mercury, Venus, Minerva, and the rest, they were themselves by no means exempt from the delusions of Satan; and, as we have already remarked, whatever subterfuges their ingenuity has invented, none of the philosophers can exculpate themselves from the crime of revolting from God by the corruption of his truth. For this reason Habakkuk, after condemning all idols, bids us to seek "the Lord in his holy temple," that the faithful might acknowledge no other God than Jehovah, who had revealed himself in his word.

3.

God Contradistinguished from Idols, that He May Be Solely and Supremely Worshipped.

We said, at the beginning, that the knowledge of God consists not in frigid speculation, but is accompanied by the worship of him. We also cursorily touched on the right method of worshipping him, which will be more fully explained in other places. I now only repeat, in few words, that whenever the Scripture asserts that there is but one God, it contends not for the bare name, but also teaches, that whatever belongs to the Deity, should not be transferred to another. This shows how pure religion differs from idolatry. The Greek word ευσεβεια certainly signifies right worship, since even blind mortals, groping in the dark, have always perceived the necessity of some certain rule, that the worship of God may not be involved in disorder and confusion. Although Cicero ingeniously and correctly derives the word *religion* from a verb signifying "to read over again," or "to gather again;" yet the reason he assigns for it, that good worshippers often recollect, and diligently reconsider what is true, is forced and far-fetched. I rather think the word is opposed to a liberty of wandering without restraint; because the greater part of the world rashly embraces whatever they meet with, and also ramble from one thing to another; but piety, in order to walk with a steady step, collects itself within its proper limits. The word *superstition* also appears to me to import a discontent with the method and order prescribed, and an accumulation of a superfluous mass of vain things. But to leave the consideration of words, it has been generally admitted, in all ages, that religion is corrupted and perverted by errors and falsehoods; whence we infer, that when we allow ourselves anything from inconsiderate zeal, the pretext alleged by the superstitious is altogether frivolous. Although this confession is in the mouths of all, they betray, at the same time, a shameful ignorance, neither adhering to the one true God, nor observing any discrimination in his worship, as we have before shown. But God, to assert his own right, proclaims that he is "jealous," and will be a severe avenger, if men confound him with any fictitious deity; and then, to retain mankind in obedience, he defines his legitimate worship. He comprises both in his law, where he first binds the faithful to himself, as their sole legislator; and then prescribes a rule for the right worship of him according to his will. Now, of the law, since the uses and ends of it are various, I shall treat in its proper place: at present, I only remark, that it sets up a barrier to prevent men turning aside to corrupt modes of worship. Let us remember, what I have already stated, that, unless every thing belonging to Divinity remain in God alone, he is spoiled of his honour, and his worship is violated. And here it is necessary to animadvert more particularly on the subtle fallacies of superstition. For it revolts not to strange gods, in such a manner as to appear to desert the supreme God, or to degrade him to a level with others; but, allowing him the highest place, it surrounds him with a multitude of inferior deities, among whom it distributes his honours; and thus, in a cunning and hypocritical manner, the glory of Divinity is divided among many, instead of remaining wholly in one. Thus the ancient idolaters, Jews as well as Gentiles, imagined one God, the Father and Governor of all, and subordinate to him a vast multitude of other deities; to whom, in common with the supreme God, they attributed the government of heaven and earth.

Thus the saints, who departed out of this life some ages ago, are exalted to the society of God, to be worshipped, and invoked, and celebrated like him. We suppose, indeed, the glory of God not to be sullied with this abomination; whereas it is, in a great measure, suppressed and extinguished, except that we retain some faint notion of his supreme power; but, at the same time, deceived with such impostures, we are seduced to the worship of various deities.

II. On this account was invented the distinction of *latria* and *dulia*, as they express themselves, by which they conceived they might safely ascribe divine honours to angels and deceased men. For it is evident, that the worship which papists pay to the saints, differs not in reality from the worship of God; for they adore God and them promiscuously; but when they are accused of it, they evade the charge with this subterfuge, that they preserve inviolate to God what belongs to him, because they leave him λατρεια. But since the question relates to a thing, not to a word, who can bear their careless trifling on the most important of all subjects? But, to pass this also, they will gain nothing at last by their distinction, but that they render worship to God alone, and service to the saints. For λατρεια, in Greek, signifies the same as *cultus* in Latin, [and *worship* in English;] but δουλεια properly signifies *servitus*, [*service*;] and yet, in the Scriptures, this distinction is sometimes disregarded. But, suppose it to be a constant distinction, it remains to be inquired, what is the meaning of each term. Λατρεια is *worship*; δουλεια is *service*. Now, no one doubts, that to serve is more than to worship or honour. For it would be irksome to serve many persons, whom you would not refuse to honour. So unjust is the distribution, to assign the greater to the saints, and leave to God that which is less. But many of the ancients, it is urged, have used this distinction. What is that to the purpose, if every one perceives it to be not only improper, but altogether frivolous?

III. Leaving these subtleties, let us consider the subject itself. Paul, when he reminds the Galatians what they had been before they were illuminated in the knowledge of God, says, that they "did service to them which by nature were no gods." Though he mentions not λατρεια, (worship,) is their idolatry therefore excusable? He certainly condemns that perverse superstition, which he denominates δουλεια, (service,) equally as much as if he had used the word λατρεια, (worship.) And when Christ repels the assault of Satan with this shield, "It is written, Thou shalt worship the Lord thy God," the word λατρεια came not into the question; for Satan required nothing but προσκυνησις, (prostration, or adoration.) So, when John is reprehended by an angel, for having fallen on his knees before him, we must not understand that John was so stupid as to intend to transfer to an angel the honour due exclusively to God. But since all worship, that is connected with religion, cannot but savour of Divine, he could not (προσκυνειν) prostrate himself before the angel, without detracting from the glory of God. We read, indeed, frequently, of men having been worshipped; but that was civil honour, so to speak; religion has a different design; and no sooner is religion connected with worship, or homage, than it produces a profanation of the Divine honour. We may see the same in Cornelius, who had not made such a small progress in piety, as not to ascribe supreme worship to God alone. When he "fell down" before Peter, therefore, it certainly was not with an intention of worshipping him instead of God: yet Peter positively forbade him to do it. And why was this, but because men never so particularly distinguish between the worship or homage of God, and that of the creatures, as to avoid transferring to a creature what belongs exclusively to God? Wherefore, if we desire to have but one God, let us remember, that his glory ought not, in the least, to be diminished; but that he must retain all that belongs to him. Therefore Zechariah, when speaking of the restoration of the Church, expressly declares, not only that "there shall be one Lord," but also "that his name shall be one;" signifying, without doubt, that he will have nothing in common with idols. Now, what kind of worship God requires, will be seen, in due course, in another place. For he hath been pleased, in his law, to prescribe to mankind what is lawful and right; and so to confine them to a certain rule, that every individual might not take the liberty of inventing a mode of worship according to his own fancy. But, since it is not proper to burden the reader, by confounding many subjects together, I shall not enter on that point yet; let it suffice to know, that no religious services can be transferred to any other than God alone, without committing sacrilege. At first, indeed, superstition ascribed Divine honours either to the sun, or to the other stars, or to idols. Afterwards followed ambition, which, adorning men with the spoils of God, dared to profane everything that was sacred. And although there remained a persuasion, that they ought to worship a supreme God, yet it became customary to offer sacrifices promiscuously to genii, and inferior deities, and deceased heroes. So steep is the descent to this vice, to communicate to a vast multitude that which God particularly challenges to himself alone!

4.

One Divine Essence, Containing Three Persons; Taught in the Scriptures from the Beginning.

What is taught in the Scriptures concerning the immensity and spirituality of the essence of God, should serve not only to overthrow the foolish notions of the vulgar, but also to refute the subtleties of profane philosophy. One of the ancients, in his own conception very shrewdly, said, that whatever we see, and whatever we do not see, is God. But he imagined that the Deity was diffused through every part of the world. But, although God, to keep us within the bounds of sobriety, speaks but rarely of his essence, yet, by those two attributes, which I have mentioned, he supersedes all gross imaginations, and represses the presumption of the human mind. For, surely, his immensity ought to inspire us with awe, that we may not attempt to measure him with our senses; and the spirituality of his nature prohibits us from entertaining any earthly or carnal speculations concerning him. For the same reason, he represents his residence to be "in heaven;" for though, as he is incomprehensible, he fills the earth also; yet, seeing that our minds, from their dulness, are continually dwelling on the earth, in order to shake off our sloth and inactivity, he properly raises us above the world. And here is demolished the error of the Manichees, who, by maintaining the existence of two original principles, made the devil, as it were, equal to God. This certainly was both dividing the unity of God, and limiting his immensity. For their daring to abuse certain testimonies of Scripture betrayed a shameful ignorance; as the error itself evidenced an execrable madness. The Anthropomorphites also, who imagined God to be corporeal, because the Scripture frequently ascribes to him a mouth, ears, eyes, hands, and feet, are easily refuted. For who, even of the meanest capacity, understands not, that God lisps, as it were, with us, just as nurses are accustomed to speak to infants? Wherefore, such forms of expression do not clearly explain the nature of God, but accommodate the knowledge of him to our narrow capacity; to accomplish which, the Scripture must necessarily descend far below the height of his majesty.

II. But he also designates himself by another peculiar character, by which he may be yet more clearly distinguished; for, while he declares himself to be but One, he proposes himself to be distinctly considered in Three Persons, without apprehending which, we have only a bare and empty name of God floating in our brains, without any idea of the true God. Now, that no one may vainly dream of three gods, or suppose that the simple essence of God is divided among the three Persons, we must seek for a short and easy definition, which will preserve us from all error. But since some violently object to the word Person, as of human invention, we must first examine the reasonableness of this objection. When the Apostle denominates the Son the express image of the hypostasis of the Father, he undoubtedly ascribes to the Father some subsistence, in which he differs from the Son. For to understand this word as synonymous with Essence, (as some interpreters have done, as though Christ, like wax impressed with a seal, represented in himself the substance of the Father,) were not only harsh, but also absurd. For the essence of God being simple and indivisible, he who contains all in himself, not in part, or by derivation, but in complete perfection, could not, without impropriety, and even absurdity, be called the express image of it. But since the Father, although distinguished by his own peculiar property, hath expressed himself entirely in his Son, it is with the greatest reason asserted that he hath made his hypostasis conspicuous in him; with which the other appellation, given him in the same passage, of "the brightness of his glory," exactly corresponds. From the words of the Apostle, we certainly conclude, that there is in the Father a proper hypostasis, which is conspicuous in the Son. And thence also we easily infer the hypostasis of the Son, which distinguishes him from the Father. The same reasoning is applicable to the Holy Spirit; for we shall soon prove him also to be God; and yet he must, of necessity, be considered as distinct from the Father. But this is not a distinction of the essence, which it is unlawful to represent as any other than simple and undivided. It follows, therefore, if the testimony of the Apostle be credited, that there are in God three *hypostases*. And, as the Latins have expressed the same thing by the word *person*, it is too fastidious and obstinate to contend about so clear a matter. If we wish to translate word for word, we may call it *subsistence*. Many, in the same sense, have called it *substance*. Nor has the word *person* been used by the Latins only; but the Greeks also, for the sake of testifying their consent to this doctrine, taught the existence of three προσωπα (persons) in God. But both Greeks and Latins, notwithstanding any verbal difference, are in perfect harmony respecting the doctrine itself.

III. Now, though heretics rail at the word *person*, or some morose and obstinate men clamorously refuse to admit a name of human invention; since they cannot make us assert that there are three, each of whom is entirely God, nor yet that there are more gods than one, how very unreasonable is it to reprobate words which express nothing but what is testified and recorded in the Scriptures! It were better, say they, to restrain not only our thoughts, but our expressions also, within the limits of the Scripture, than to introduce exotic words, which may generate future dissensions and disputes; for thus we weary ourselves with verbal controversies; thus the truth is lost in altercation; thus charity expires in odious contention. If they call every word exotic, which cannot be found in the Scriptures in so many syllables, they impose on us a law which is very unreasonable, and which condemns all interpretation, but what is composed of detached texts of Scripture connected together. But if by exotic they mean that which is curiously contrived, and superstitiously defended, which tends to contention more than to edification, the use of which is either unseasonable or unprofitable, which offends pious ears with its harshness, and seduces persons from the simplicity of the Divine word, I most cordially embrace their modest opinion. For I think that we ought to speak of God with the same religious caution, which should govern our thoughts of him; since all the thoughts that we entertain concerning him merely from ourselves, are foolish, and all our expressions absurd. But there is a proper medium to be observed: we should seek in the Scriptures a certain rule, both for thinking and for speaking; by which we may regulate all the thoughts of our minds, and all the words of our mouths. But what forbids our expressing, in plainer words, those things which, in the Scriptures, are, to our understanding, intricate and obscure, provided our expressions religiously and faithfully convey the true sense of the Scripture, and are used with modest caution, and not without sufficient occasion? Of this, examples sufficiently numerous are not wanting. But, when it shall have been proved, that the Church was absolutely necessitated to use the terms Trinity and Persons, if any one then censures the novelty of the words, may he not be justly considered as offended at the light of the truth? as having no other cause of censure, but that the truth is explained and elucidated?

IV. But such verbal novelty (if it must have this appellation) is principally used, when the truth is to be asserted in opposition to malicious cavillers, who elude it by crafty evasions; of which we have too much experience in the present day, who find great difficulty in refuting the enemies of pure and sound doctrine: possessed of serpentine lubricity, they escape by the most artful expedients, unless they are vigorously pursued, and held fast when once caught. Thus the ancients, pestered with various controversies against erroneous dogmas, were constrained to express their sentiments with the utmost perspicuity, that they might leave no subterfuges to the impious, who availed themselves of obscure expressions, for the concealment of their errors. Unable to resist the clear testimonies of the Scriptures, Arius confessed Christ to be God, and the Son of God; and, as though this were all that was necessary, he pretended to agree with the Church at large. But, at the same time, he continued to maintain that Christ was created, and had a beginning like other creatures. To draw the versatile subtlety of this man from its concealment, the ancient Fathers proceeded further, and declared Christ to be the eternal Son of the Father, and consubstantial with the Father. Here impiety openly discovered itself, when the Arians began inveterately to hate and execrate the name ὁμοούσιος, (consubstantial.) But if, in the first instance, they had sincerely and cordially confessed Christ to be God, they would not have denied him to be consubstantial with the Father. Who can dare to censure those good men, as quarrelsome and contentious, for having kindled such a flame of controversy, and disturbed the peace of the Church on account of one little word? That little word distinguished Christians, who held the pure faith, from sacrilegious Arians. Afterwards arose Sabellius, who considered the names of Father, Son, and Holy Spirit, as little more than empty sounds; arguing, that they were not used on account of any real distinction, but were different attributes of God, whose attributes of this kind are numerous. If the point came to be controverted, he confessed, that he believed the Father to be God, the Son God, and the Holy Spirit God; but he would readily evade all the force of this confession, by adding, that he had said no other than if he had called God potent, and just, and wise. And thus he came to another conclusion, that the Father is the Son, and that the Holy Spirit is the Father, without any order or distinction. The good doctors of that age, who had the interest of religion at heart, in order to counteract the wickedness of this man, maintained, on the contrary, that they ought really to acknowledge three peculiar properties in one God. And, to defend themselves against his intricate subtleties, by the plain and simple truth, they affirmed, that they truly subsisted in the one God; or, what is the same, that in the unity of God there subsisted a trinity of Persons.

V. If, then, the words have not been rashly invented, we should beware lest we be convicted of fastidious temerity in rejecting them. I could wish them, indeed, to be buried in oblivion, provided this faith were universally received, that the Father, Son, and Holy Spirit, are the one God; and that nevertheless the Son is not the Father, nor the Spirit the Son, but that they are distinguished from each other by some peculiar property. I am not so rigidly precise as to be fond of contending for mere words. For I observe that the ancients, who otherwise speak on these subjects with great piety, are not consistent with each other, nor, in all cases, with themselves. For what forms of expression, adopted by councils, does Hilary excuse! To what extremes does

Augustine sometimes proceed! How different are the Greeks from the Latins! But of this variation, let one example suffice: when the Latins would translate the word ὁμοούσιος, they called it *consubstantial*, signifying the *substance* of the Father and the Son to be one, and thus using *substance* for *essence*. Whence also Jerome, writing to Damasus, pronounces it to be sacrilege to say that there are three *substances* in God. Yet, that there are three *substances* in God, you will find asserted in Hilary more than a hundred times. But how perplexed is Jerome on the word *hypostasis*! For he suspects some latent poison in the assertion, that there are three *hypostases* in God. And if any one uses this word in a pious sense, he refrains not from calling it an improper expression; if, indeed, he was sincere in this declaration, and did not rather knowingly and wilfully endeavour to asperse, with a groundless calumny, the bishops of the East, whom he hated. He certainly discovers not much ingenuousness in affirming that, in all the profane schools, οὐσία (essence) is the same as ὑπόστασις, (hypostasis,) which the trite and common use of the words universally contradicts. More modesty and liberality are discovered by Augustine, who, though he asserts that the word *hypostasis*, in this sense, is new to Latin ears, yet leaves the Greeks their usual phraseology, and even peaceably tolerates the Latins, who had imitated their language; and the account of Socrates, in the sixth book of his Tripartite History, seems to imply, that it was by ignorant men that it had first been improperly applied to this subject. The same Hilary accuses the heretics of a great crime, in constraining him, by their wickedness, to expose to the danger of human language those things which ought to be confined within the religion of the mind; plainly avowing that this is to do things unlawful, to express things inexpressible, to assume things not conceded. A little after, he largely excuses himself for his boldness in bringing forward new terms; for, when he has used the names of nature, Father, Son, and Spirit, he immediately adds, that whatever is sought further, is beyond the signification of language, beyond the reach of our senses, beyond the conception of our understanding. And, in another place, he pronounces that happy were the bishops of Gaul, who had neither composed, nor received, nor even known, any other confession but that ancient and very simple one, which had been received in all the churches from the days of the Apostles. Very similar is the excuse of Augustine, that this word was extorted by necessity, on account of the poverty of human language on so great a subject, not for the sake of expressing what God is, but to avoid passing it over in total silence, that the Father, Son, and Spirit are three. This moderation of those holy men should teach us, not to pass such severe censures on those who are unwilling to subscribe to expressions adopted by us, provided they are not actuated by pride, perverseness, or disingenuous subtlety. But let them also, on the other hand, consider the great necessity which constrains us to use such language, that, by degrees, they may at length be accustomed to a useful phraseology. Let them also learn to beware, since we have to oppose the Arians on one side, and the Sabellians on the other, lest, while they take offence at both these parties being deprived of all opportunity of evasion, they cause some suspicion that they are themselves the disciples either of Arius or of Sabellius. Arius confesses, "that Christ is God;" but maintains also, "that he was created, and had a beginning." He acknowledges that Christ is "one with the Father;" but secretly whispers in the ears of his disciples, that he is "united to him," like the rest of the faithful, though by a singular privilege. Say that he is *consubstantial*, you tear off the mask from the hypocrite, and yet you add nothing to the Scriptures. Sabellius asserts, "that the names Father, Son, and Spirit, are expressive of no distinction in the Godhead." Say that they are three, and he will exclaim, that you are talking of "three gods." Say, "that in the one essence of God there is a trinity of Persons," and you will at once express what the Scriptures declare, and will restrain such frivolous loquacity. Now, if any persons are prevented, by such excessive scrupulousness, from admitting these terms, yet not one of them can deny, that, when the Scripture speaks of one God, it should be understood of a unity of substance; and that, when it speaks of three in one essence, it denotes the Persons in this trinity. When this is honestly confessed, we have no further concern about words. But I have found, by long and frequent experience, that those who pertinaciously contend about words, cherish some latent poison; so that it were better designedly to provoke their resentment, than to use obscure language for the sake of obtaining their favour.

VI. But, leaving the dispute about terms, I shall now enter on the discussion of the subject itself. What I denominate a Person, is a subsistence in the Divine essence, which is related to the others, and yet distinguished from them by an incommunicable property. By the word *subsistence* we mean something different from the word *essence*. For, if the *Word* were simply God, and had no peculiar property, John had been guilty of impropriety in saying that he was always *with God*. When he immediately adds, that *the Word* also *was God*, he reminds us of the unity of the essence. But because he could not be *with God*, without subsisting in the Father, hence arises that subsistence, which, although inseparably connected with the essence, has a peculiar mark, by which it is distinguished from it. Now, I say that each of the three subsistences has a relation to the others, but is distinguished from them by a peculiar property. We particularly use the word *relation*, (or *comparison*,) here, because, when mention is made simply and indefinitely of God, this name pertains no less to the Son and Spirit, than to the Father. But whenever the Father is compared with the Son, the property peculiar to each distinguishes him from the other. Thirdly, whatever is proper to each of them, I assert to be incommunicable, because whatever is ascribed to the Father as a character of distinction, cannot be applied or transferred to the Son. Nor, indeed, do I disapprove of the definition of Tertullian, if rightly understood: "That there is in God a certain distribution or economy, which makes no change in the unity of the essence."

VII. But before I proceed any further, I must prove the Deity of the Son and of the Holy Spirit; after which we shall see how they differ from each other. When the Scripture speaks of *the Word of God*, it certainly were very absurd to imagine it to be only a transient and momentary sound, emitted into the air, and coming forth from God himself; of which nature were the oracles, given to the fathers, and all the prophecies. It is rather to be understood of the eternal wisdom residing in God, whence the oracles, and all the prophecies, proceeded. For, according to the testimony of Peter, the ancient Prophets spake by the Spirit of Christ no less than the Apostles and all the succeeding ministers of the heavenly doctrine. But, as Christ had not yet been manifested, we must necessarily understand that the Word was begotten of the Father before the world began. And if the Spirit that inspired the Prophets was the Spirit of the Word, we conclude, beyond all doubt, that the Word was truly God. And this is taught by Moses, with sufficient perspicuity, in the creation of the world, in which he represents the Word as acting such a conspicuous part. For why does he relate that God, in the creation of each of his works, said, Let this or that be done, but that the unsearchable glory of God may resplendently appear in his image? Captious and loquacious men would readily evade this argument, by saying, that the *Word* imports an order or command; but the

Apostles are better interpreters, who declare, that the worlds were created by the Son, and that he "upholds all things by the word of his power." For here we see that the *Word* intends the nod or mandate of the Son, who is himself the eternal and essential Son of the Father. Nor, to the wise and sober, is there any obscurity in that passage of Solomon, where he introduces Wisdom as begotten of the Father before time began, and presiding at the creation of the world, and over all the works of God. For, to pretend that this denotes some temporary expression of the will of God, were foolish and frivolous; whereas God then intended to discover his fixed and eternal counsel, and even something more secret. To the same purpose also is that assertion of Christ, "My Father worketh hitherto, and I work." For, by affirming that, from the beginning of the world, he had continually cooperated with the Father, he makes a more explicit declaration of what had been briefly glanced at by Moses. We conclude, therefore, that God spake thus at the creation, that the Word might have his part in the work, and so that operation be common to both. But John speaks more clearly than all others, when he represents *the Word*, who from the beginning *was God with God*, as in union with the Father, the original cause of all things. For to the Word he both attributes a real and permanent essence, and assigns some peculiar property; and plainly shows how God, by speaking, created the world. Therefore, as all Divine revelations are justly entitled *the word of God*, so we ought chiefly to esteem that substantial Word the source of all revelations, who is liable to no variation, who remains with God perpetually one and the same, and who is God himself.

VIII. Here we are interrupted by some clamorous objectors, who, since they cannot openly rob him of his divinity, secretly steal from him his eternity. For they say, that the Word only began to exist, when God opened his sacred mouth in the creation of the world. But they are too inconsiderate in imagining something new in the substance of God. For, as those names of God, which relate to his external works, began to be ascribed to him after the existence of those works, as when he is called the Creator of heaven and earth, so piety neither acknowledges nor admits any name, signifying that God has found any thing new to happen to himself. For, could any thing, from any quarter, effect a change in him, it would contradict the assertion of James, that "every good gift and every perfect gift is from above, and cometh down from the Father of lights, with whom is no variableness or shadow of turning." Nothing, then, is more intolerable, than to suppose a beginning of that Word, which was always God, and afterwards the Creator of the world. But they argue, in their own apprehension most acutely, that Moses, by representing God as having then spoken for the first time, implies also, that there was no Word in him before; than which nothing is more absurd. For it is not to be concluded, because any thing begins to be manifested at a certain time, that it had no prior existence. I form a very different conclusion; that, since, in the very instant when God said, "Let there be light," the power of the Word was clearly manifested, the Word must have existed long before. But if any one inquires, how long, he will find no beginning. For he limits no certain period of time, when he himself says, "O Father, glorify thou me with thine own self, with the glory which I had with thee before the world was." Nor is this omitted by John; for, before he descends to the creation of the world, he declares that the Word "was in the beginning with God." We therefore conclude again, that the Word, conceived of God before time began, perpetually remained with him, which proves his eternity, his true essence, and his divinity.

IX. Though I advert not yet to the person of the Mediator, but defer it to that part of the work which will relate to redemption, yet, since it ought, without controversy, to be believed by all, that Christ is the very same Word clothed in flesh, any testimonies which assert the Deity of Christ, will be very properly introduced here. When it is said, in the forty-fifth Psalm, "Thy throne, O God, is for ever and ever," the Jews endeavour to evade its force, by pleading that the name Elohim is applicable also to angels, and to men of dignity and power. But there cannot be found in the Scripture a similar passage, which erects an eternal throne for a creature; for he is not merely called God, but is also declared to possess an eternal dominion. Besides, this title is never given to a creature, without some addition, as when it is said that Moses should be "a god to Pharaoh." Some read it in the genitive case, "Thy throne is of God," which is extremely insipid. I confess, indeed, that what is eminently and singularly excellent, is frequently called Divine; but it sufficiently appears from the context, that such a meaning would be uncouth and forced, and totally inapplicable here. But, if their perverseness refuse to yield this point, there certainly is no obscurity in Isaiah, where he introduces Christ as God, and as crowned with supreme power, which is the prerogative of God alone. "His name," says he, "shall be called the Mighty God, the Father of eternity," &c. Here also the Jews object, and invert the reading of the passage in this manner: "This is the name by which the mighty God, the Father of eternity, shall call him," &c.; so that they would leave the Son only the title of Prince of peace. But to what purpose would so many epithets be accumulated in this passage on God the Father, when the design of the prophet is to distinguish Christ by such eminent characters as may establish our faith in him? Wherefore, there can be no doubt that he is there denominated the Mighty God, just as, a little before, he is called Immanuel. But nothing can be required plainer than a passage in Jeremiah, that this should be the name whereby the Branch of David shall be called "Jehovah our righteousness." For since the Jews themselves teach, that all other names of God are mere epithets, but that this alone, which they call ineffable, is a proper name expressive of his Essence, we conclude, that the Son is the one eternal God, who declares, in another place, that he "will not give his glory to another." This also they endeavour to evade, because Moses imposed this name on an altar which he built, and Ezekiel on the city of the new Jerusalem. But who does not perceive, that the altar was erected as a monument of Moses having been exalted by God, and that Jerusalem is honoured with the name of God, only as a testimony of the Divine presence? For thus speaks the prophet: "The name of the city shall be, Jehovah is there." But Moses expresses himself thus: He "built an altar, and called the name of it Jehovah-nissi," (my exaltation.) But there is more contention about another passage of Jeremiah, where the same title is given to Jerusalem in these words: "This is the name wherewith she shall be called, Jehovah our righteousness." But this testimony is so far from opposing the truth which we are defending, that it rather confirms it. For, having before testified that Christ is the true Jehovah, from whom righteousness proceeds, he now pronounces that the church will have such a clear apprehension of it, as to be able to glory in the same name. In the former place, then, is shown the original cause of righteousness, in the latter the effect.

X. Now, if these things do not satisfy the Jews, I see not by what cavils they can evade the accounts of Jehovah having so frequently appeared in the character of an angel. An angel is said to have appeared to the holy fathers. He claims for himself the name of the eternal God. If it be objected, that this is spoken with regard to the character which he sustains, this by no means removes the difficulty. For a servant would never rob God of his honour, by permitting sacrifice to be offered to himself. But the angel, refusing to eat bread, commands a sacrifice to be offered to Jehovah. He afterwards demonstrates that he is really Jehovah himself. Therefore Manoah and his wife conclude, from this evidence, that they have seen, not a mere angel, but God himself. Hence he says, "We shall surely die, because we have seen God." When his wife replies, "If the Lord were pleased to kill us, he would not have received" a sacrifice "at our hands," she clearly acknowledges him to be God, who before is called an angel. Moreover, the reply of the angel himself removes every doubt: "Why askest thou after my name, seeing it is wonderful?" So much the more detestable is the impiety of Servetus, in asserting that God never appeared to Abraham and the other patriarchs, but that they worshipped an angel in his stead. But the orthodox doctors of the church have truly and wisely understood and taught, that the same chief angel was the Word of God, who even then began to perform some services introductory to his execution of the office of Mediator. For though he was not yet incarnate, he descended, as it were, in a mediatorial capacity, that he might approach the faithful with greater familiarity. His familiar intercourse with men gave him the name of an angel; yet he still retained what properly belonged to him, and continued the ineffably glorious God. The same truth is attested by Hosea, who, after relating the wrestling of Jacob with an angel, says, "The Lord (Jehovah) God of hosts; Jehovah is his memorial." Servetus again cavils, that God employed the person of an angel; as though the prophet did not confirm what had been delivered by Moses,—"Wherefore is it that thou dost ask after my name?" And the confession of the holy patriarch, when he says, "I have seen God face to face," sufficiently declares, that he was not a created angel, but one in whom resided the fulness of Deity. Hence, also, the representation of Paul, that Christ was the conductor of the people in the wilderness; because, though the time of his humiliation was not yet arrived, the eternal Word then exhibited a type of the office to which he was appointed. Now, if the second chapter of Zechariah be strictly and coolly examined, the angel who sends another angel is immediately pronounced the God of hosts, and supreme power is ascribed to him. I omit testimonies innumerable on which our faith safely rests, although they have little influence on the Jews. For when it is said in Isaiah, "Lo, this is our God; we have waited for him, and he will save us; this is Jehovah;" all who have eyes may perceive that this is God, who arises for the salvation of his people. And the emphatical repetition of these pointed expressions forbids an application of this passage to any other than to Christ. But still more plain and decisive is a passage of Malachi, where he prophesies, that "the Lord, who was then sought, should come into his temple." The temple was exclusively consecrated to the one Most High God; yet the prophet claims it as belonging to Christ. Whence it follows, that he is the same God that was always worshipped among the Jews.

XI. The New Testament abounds with innumerable testimonies. We must, therefore, endeavour briefly to select a few, rather than to collect them all. Though the Apostles spake of him after he had appeared in flesh as the Mediator, yet all that I shall adduce will be adapted to prove his eternal Deity. In the first place, it is worthy of particular observation, that the apostle represents those things which were predicted concerning the eternal God, as either already exhibited in Christ, or to be accomplished in him at some future period. The prediction of Isaiah, that the Lord of Hosts would be "for a stone of stumbling, and for a rock of offence to both the houses of Israel," Paul asserts to have been fulfilled in Christ. Therefore he declares, that Christ is the Lord of Hosts. There is a similar instance in another place: "We shall all stand," says he, "before the judgment-seat of Christ. For it is written, As I live, saith the Lord, every knee shall bow to me, and every tongue shall confess to God." Since God, in Isaiah, declares this concerning himself, and Christ actually exhibits it in his own person, it follows, that he is that very God, whose glory cannot be transferred to another. The apostle's quotation from the Psalms also, in his Epistle to the Ephesians, is evidently applicable to none but God: "When he ascended up on high, he led captivity captive:" understanding that ascension to have been prefigured by the exertions of the Divine power in the signal victories of David over the heathen nations, he signifies, that the text was more fully accomplished in Christ. Thus John attests that it was the glory of the Son which was revealed in a vision to Isaiah; whereas the prophet himself records that he saw the majesty of God. And those praises which the Apostle, in the Epistle to the Hebrews, ascribes to the Son, beyond all doubt most evidently belong to God: "Thou, Lord, in the beginning, hast laid the foundation of the earth; and the heavens are the works of thine hands," &c. Again, "Let all the angels of God worship him." Nor is it any misapplication of them, when he refers them to Christ; since all that is predicted in those Psalms has been accomplished only by him. For it was He who arose and had mercy upon Zion; it was He who claimed as his own the dominion over all nations and islands. And why should John, after having affirmed, at the commencement of his Gospel, that the Word was always God, have hesitated to attribute to Christ the majesty of God? And why should Paul have been afraid to place Christ on the tribunal of God, after having so publicly preached his Divinity, when he called him "God blessed for ever?" And, to show how consistent he is with himself on this subject, he says, also, that "God was manifest in the flesh." If he is "God blessed for ever," he is the same to whom this apostle, in another place, affirms all glory and honour to be due. And he conceals not, but openly proclaims, that, "being in the form of God," he "thought it not robbery to be equal with God, but made himself of no reputation." And, lest the impious might object, that he is a sort of artificial God, John goes further, and affirms, that "This is the true God, and eternal life;" although we ought to be fully satisfied by his being called God, especially by a witness who expressly avers that there are no more gods than one; I mean Paul, who says, "though there be that are called gods, whether in heaven or in earth; to us there is but one God, of whom are all things." When we hear, from the same mouth, that "God was manifested in the flesh," that "God hath purchased the Church with his own blood,"—why do we imagine a second God, whom he by no means acknowledges? And there is no doubt that all the pious were of the same opinion. Thomas, likewise, by publicly confessing him to be "his Lord and God," declares him to be the same true God whom he had always worshipped.

XII. If we judge of his Divinity from the works which the Scriptures attribute to him, it will thence appear with increasing evidence. For when he said, that he had, from the beginning, continually coöperated with the Father, the Jews, stupid as they were about his other declarations, yet perceived, that he assumed to himself Divine power; and, therefore, as John informs us, they "sought the more to kill him; because he not only had broken the sabbath, but said also that God was his Father, making himself equal with God." How great, then, must be our stupidity, if we perceive not this passage to be a plain assertion of his Divinity! To preside over the world by his almighty providence, and to govern all things by the rod of his own power, (which the Apostle attributes to him,) belongs exclusively to the Creator. And he participates with the Father, not only in the government of the world, but also in all other offices, which cannot be communicated to creatures. The Lord proclaims, by the prophet, "I, even I, am he that blotteth out thy transgressions, for mine own sake." According to this declaration, when the Jews thought that Christ committed an injury against God, by undertaking to forgive sins, he not only asserted in express terms, that this power belonged to him, but proved it by a miracle. We see, therefore, that he hath not the ministry, but the power of remission of sins, which the Lord declares shall never be transferred from himself to another. Is it not the prerogative of God alone to examine and penetrate the secret thoughts of the heart? Yet Christ possessed that power; which is a proof of his Divinity.

XIII. But with what perspicuity of evidence does it appear in his miracles! Though I grant that the Prophets and Apostles performed miracles similar and equal to his, yet there is a considerable difference in this respect, that they, in their ministry, dispensed the favours of God, whereas his miracles were performed by his exertions of his own power. He sometimes, indeed, used prayer, that he might glorify the Father; but, in most instances, we perceive the manifest displays of his own power. And how should not he be the true author of miracles, who, by his own authority, committed the dispensation of them to others? For the Evangelists relate, that he gave his Apostles power to raise the dead, to heal the leprous, to cast out devils, &c. And they performed that ministry in such a manner, as plainly to discover, that the power proceeded solely from Christ. "In the name of Jesus Christ," says Peter, "arise and walk." It is no wonder, therefore, that Christ should bring forward his miracles, to convince the incredulity of the Jews, since, being performed by his own power, they afforded most ample evidence of his Divinity. Besides, if out of God there be no salvation, no righteousness, no life, but Christ contains all these things in himself, it certainly demonstrates him to be God. Let it not be objected, that life and salvation are infused into him by God; for he is not said to have received salvation, but to be himself salvation. And if no one be good but God alone, how can he be a mere man who is, I will not say good and righteous, but goodness and righteousness itself? Even from the beginning of the creation, according to the testimony of an Evangelist, "in him was life; and the life" then existed as "the light of men." Supported by such proofs, therefore, we venture to repose our faith and hope on him; whereas we know that it is impious and sacrilegious for any man to place his confidence in creatures. He says, "Ye believe in God, believe also in me." And in this sense Paul interprets two passages of Isaiah—"Whosoever believeth on him shall not be ashamed." Again, "There shall be a root of Jesse, that shall rise to reign over the Gentiles; in him shall the Gentiles trust." And why should we search for more testimonies from Scripture, when this declaration occurs so frequently, "He that believeth on me hath everlasting life"? The invocation, arising from faith, is also directed to him; which, nevertheless, peculiarly belongs, if any thing peculiarly belongs, to the Divine majesty. For a prophet says, "Whosoever shall call on the name of the Lord (Jehovah) shall be delivered." And Solomon, "The name of the Lord is a strong tower: the righteous runneth into it, and is safe." But the name of Christ is invoked for salvation: it follows, therefore, that he is Jehovah. Moreover, we have an example of such invocation in Stephen, when he says, "Lord Jesus, receive my spirit." And afterwards in the whole Church, as Ananias testifies in the same book: "Lord,

I have heard by many of this man, how much evil he hath done to thy saints—that call on thy name." And to make it more clearly understood, that "all the fulness of the Godhead dwelleth bodily in Christ," the Apostle confesses that he had introduced among the Corinthians no other doctrine than the knowledge of him, and that this had been the only subject of his preaching. What a remarkable and important consideration is it, that the name of the Son only is preached to us, whereas God commands us to glory in the knowledge of himself alone! Who can dare to assert that he is a mere creature, the knowledge of whom is our only glory? It must also be remarked, that the salutations prefixed to the epistles of Paul implore the same blessings from the Son as from the Father; whence we learn, not only that those things, which our heavenly Father bestows, are obtained for us by his intercession, but that the Son, by a communion of power, is himself the author of them. This practical knowledge is unquestionably more certain and solid than any idle speculation. For then the pious mind has the nearest view of the Divine presence, and almost touches it, when it experiences itself to be quickened, illuminated, saved, justified, and sanctified.

XIV. Wherefore the proof of the Deity of the Spirit must be derived principally from the same sources. There is no obscurity in the testimony of Moses, in the history of the creation, that the Spirit of God was expanded on the abyss or chaos; for it signifies, not only that the beautiful state of the world which we now behold owes its preservation to the power of the Spirit, but that, previously to its being thus adorned, the Spirit was engaged in brooding over the confused mass. The declaration of Isaiah bids defiance to all cavils: "And now the Lord God, and his Spirit, hath sent me." For the Holy Spirit is united in the exercise of supreme power in the mission of Prophets, which is a proof of his Divine majesty. But the best confirmation, as I have remarked, we shall derive from familiar experience. For what the Scriptures ascribe to him, and what we ourselves learn by the certain experience of piety, is not at all applicable to any creature. For it is he who, being universally diffused, sustains and animates all things in heaven and in earth. And this very thing excludes him from the number of creatures, that he is circumscribed by no limits, but transfuses through all his own vigorous influence, to inspire them with being, life, and motion: this is clearly a work of Deity. Again, if regeneration to an incorruptible life be more important and excellent than any present life, what must we think of him from whose power it proceeds? But the Scripture teaches, in various places, that he is the author of regeneration by a power not derived, but properly his own; and not of regeneration only, but likewise of the future immortality. Finally, to him, as well as to the Son, are applied all those offices which are peculiar to Deity. For he "searcheth even the deep things of God," who admits no creature to a share in his councils. He bestows wisdom and the faculty of speech; whereas the Lord declares to Moses, that this can only be done by himself. So through him we attain to a participation of God, to feel his vivifying energy upon us. Our justification is his work. From him proceed power, sanctification, truth, grace, and every other blessing we can conceive; since there is but one Spirit, from whom every kind of gifts descends. For this passage of Paul is worthy of particular attention: "There are diversities of gifts, and there are differences of administrations, but the same Spirit;" because it represents him, not only as the principle and source of them, but also as the author; which is yet more clearly expressed a little after in these words: "All these worketh that only and the self-same Spirit, dividing to every man severally as he will." For if he were not a subsistence in the Deity, judgment and voluntary determination would never be ascribed to him. Paul, therefore, very clearly attributes to the Spirit Divine power, and thereby demonstrates him to be an hypostasis or subsistence in God.

XV. Nor does the Scripture, when it speaks of him, refrain from giving him the appellation of God. For Paul concludes that we are the temple of God, because his Spirit dwelleth in us. This must not be passed over without particular notice; for the frequent promises of God, that he will choose us for a temple for himself, receive no other accomplishment, than by the inhabitation of his Spirit in us. Certainly, as Augustine excellently observes, "If we were commanded to erect to the Spirit a temple of wood and stone, forasmuch as God is the sole object of worship, it would be a clear proof of his Divinity; how much clearer, then, is the proof, now that we are commanded, not to erect one, but to be ourselves his temples!" And the Apostle calls us sometimes the temple of God, and sometimes the temple of the Holy Spirit, both in the same signification. Peter, reprehending Ananias for having "lied to the Holy Ghost," told him that he had "not lied unto men, but unto God." And where Isaiah introduces the Lord of hosts as the speaker, Paul informs us that it is the Holy Spirit who speaks. Indeed, while the Prophets invariably declare, that the words which they utter are those of the Lord of hosts, Christ and the Apostles refer them to the Holy Spirit; whence it follows, that he is the true Jehovah, who is the primary author of the prophecies. Again, God complains that his anger was provoked by the perverseness of the people; Isaiah, in reference to the same conduct, says, that "they vexed his Holy Spirit." Lastly, if blasphemy against the Spirit be not forgiven, either in this world or in that which is to come, whilst a man may obtain pardon who has been guilty of blasphemy against the Son, this is an open declaration of his Divine majesty, to defame or degrade which is an inexpiable crime. I intentionally pass over many testimonies which were used by the fathers. To them there appeared much plausibility in citing this passage from David, "By the word of the Lord were the heavens made, and all the host of them by the breath of his mouth;" to prove that the creation of the world was the work of the Holy Spirit, as well as of the Son. But since a repetition of the same thing twice is common in the Psalms, and in Isaiah "the spirit of his mouth" means the same as "his word," this is but a weak argument. Therefore I have determined to confine myself to a sober statement of those evidences on which pious minds may satisfactorily rest.

XVI. As God afforded a clearer manifestation of himself at the advent of Christ, the three Persons also then became better known. Among many testimonies, let us be satisfied with this one: Paul connects together these three, Lord, Faith, and Baptism, in such a manner as to reason from one to another. Since there is but one faith, hence he proves that there is but one Lord; since there is but one baptism, he shows that there is also but one faith. Therefore, if we are initiated by baptism into the faith and religion of one God, we must necessarily suppose him to be the true God, into whose name we are baptized. Nor can it be doubted but that in this solemn commission, "Baptize them in the name of the Father, and of the Son, and of the Holy Ghost," Christ intended to testify, that the perfect light of faith was now exhibited. For this is equivalent to being baptized into the name of the one God, who hath clearly manifested himself in the Father, Son, and Spirit; whence it evidently appears, that in the Divine Essence there exist three Persons, in whom is known the one God. And truly, since faith ought not to be looking about hither and thither, or to be wandering through the varieties of inconstancy, but to direct its views towards the one God, to be fixed on him, and to adhere to him,—it may easily be proved from these premises, that, if there be various kinds of faith, there must also be a plurality of gods. Baptism, being a sacrament of faith, confirms to us the unity of God, because it is but one. Hence, also, we conclude, that it is not lawful to be baptized, except into the name of the one God; because we embrace the faith of him, into whose name we are baptized. What, then, was intended by Christ, when he commanded baptism to be administered in the name of the Father, and of the Son, and of the Holy Spirit, but that one faith ought to be exercised in the Father, Son, and Spirit? and what is that but a clear testimony, that the Father, the Son, and the Holy Spirit, are the one God? Therefore, since it is an undeniable truth, that there is one God, and only one, we conclude the Word and Spirit to be no other than the very Essence of the Deity. The greatest degree of folly was betrayed by the Arians, who confessed the Divinity of the Son, but denied him to possess the substance of God. Nor were the Macedonians free from a similar delusion, who would explain the term "Spirit" to mean only the gifts of grace conferred upon man. For as wisdom, understanding, prudence, fortitude, and the fear of the Lord, proceed from him, so he alone is the Spirit of wisdom, prudence, fortitude, and piety. Nor is he himself divided according to the distribution of his graces; but, as the Apostle declares, how variously soever they are divided, he always remains one and the same.

XVII. On the other hand, also, we find in the Scriptures a distinction between the Father and the Word, between the Word and the Spirit; in the discussion of which the magnitude of the mystery reminds us that we ought to proceed with the utmost reverence and sobriety. I am exceedingly pleased with this observation of Gregory Nazianzen: "I cannot think of the *one*, but I am immediately surrounded with the splendour of the *three*; nor can I clearly discover the *three*, but I am suddenly carried back to the *one*." Wherefore let us not imagine such a trinity of Persons, as includes an idea of separation, or does not immediately recall us to the unity. The names of Father, Son, and Spirit, certainly imply a real distinction; let no one suppose them to be mere epithets, by which God is variously designated from his works; but it is a distinction, not a division. The passages already cited show, that the Son has a property, by which he is distinguished from the Father; because the Word had not been with God, or had his glory with the Father, unless he had been distinct from him. He likewise distinguishes the Father from himself, when he says, "that there is another that beareth witness of him." And to the same effect is what is declared in another place, that the Father created all things by the Word; which he could not have done, unless he had been in some sense distinct from him. Besides, the Father descended not to the earth, but he who came forth from the Father. The Father neither died nor rose again, but he who was sent by the Father. Nor did this distinction commence at the incarnation, but it is evident, that, before that period, he was the only begotten in the bosom of the Father. For who can undertake to assert, that the Son first entered into the bosom of the Father, when he descended from heaven to assume a human nature? He, therefore, was in the bosom of the Father before, and possessed his glory with the Father. The distinction between the Holy Spirit and the Father is announced by Christ, when he says, that he "proceedeth from the Father." But how often does he represent him as another, distinct from himself! as when he promises that "another Comforter" should be sent, and in many other places.

XVIII. I doubt the propriety of borrowing similitudes from human things, to express the force of this distinction. The fathers sometimes practise this method; but they likewise confess the great disproportion of all the similitudes which they introduce. Wherefore I greatly dread, in this instance, every degree of presumption; lest the introduction of any thing unseasonable should afford an occasion of calumny to the malicious, or of error to the ignorant. Yet it is not right to be silent on the distinction which we find expressed in the Scriptures; which is this—that to the Father is attributed the principle of action, the fountain and source of all things; to the Son, wisdom, counsel, and the arrangement of all operations; and the power and efficacy of the action is assigned to the Spirit. Moreover, though eternity belongs to the Father, and to the Son and Spirit also, since God can never have been destitute of his wisdom or his power, and in eternity we must not inquire after any thing prior or posterior,—yet the observation of order is not vain or superfluous, while the Father is mentioned as first; in the next place the Son, as from him; and then the Spirit, as from both. For the mind of every man naturally inclines to the consideration, first, of God; secondly, of the wisdom emanating from him; and lastly, of the power by which he executes the decrees of his wisdom. For this reason the Son is said to be from the Father, and the Spirit from both the Father and the Son; and that in various places, but nowhere more clearly than in the eighth chapter of the Epistle to the Romans, where the same Spirit is indifferently denominated "the Spirit of Christ," and "the Spirit of him that raised up Christ from the dead," and that without any impropriety. For Peter also testifies that it was the Spirit of Christ by whom the prophets prophesied; whereas the Scripture so frequently declares that it was the Spirit of God the Father.

XIX. This distinction is so far from opposing the most absolute simplicity and unity of the Divine Being, that it affords a proof that the Son is one God with the Father, because he has the same Spirit with him; and that the Spirit is not a different substance from the Father and the Son, because he is the Spirit of the Father and of the Son. For the whole nature is in each hypostasis, and each has something peculiar to himself. The Father is entirely in the Son, and the Son entirely in the Father, according to his own declaration, "I am in the Father, and the Father in me;" nor do ecclesiastical writers allow that one is divided from the other by any difference of essence. "These distinctive appellations," says Augustine, "denote their reciprocal relations to each other, and not the substance itself, which is but one." This explanation may serve to reconcile the opinions of the fathers, which would otherwise appear totally repugnant to each other. For sometimes they state that the Son originates from the Father, and at other times assert that he has essential Divinity from himself, and so is, together with the Father, the one first cause of all. Augustine, in another place, admirably and perspicuously explains the cause of this diversity, in the following manner: "Christ, considered in himself, is called God; but with relation to the Father, he is called the Son." And again, "The Father, considered in himself, is called God; but with relation to the Son, he is called the Father. He who, with relation to the Son, is called the Father, is not the Son; he who, with relation to the Father, is called the Son, is not the Father; they who are severally called the Father and the Son, are the same God." Therefore, when we speak simply of the Son, without reference to the Father, we truly and properly assert him to be self-existent, and therefore call him the sole first cause; but, when we distinctly treat of the relation between him and the Father, we justly represent him as originating from the Father. The first book of Augustine on the Trinity is entirely occupied with the explication of this subject; and it is far more safe to rest satisfied with that relation which he states, than by curiously penetrating into the sublime mystery, to wander through a multitude of vain speculations.

XX. Therefore, let such as love sobriety, and will be contented with the measure of faith, briefly attend to what is useful to be known; which is, that, when we profess to believe in one God, the word *God* denotes a single and simple essence, in which we comprehend three Persons, or hypostases; and that, therefore, whenever the word *God* is used indefinitely, the Son and Spirit are intended as much as the Father; but when the Son is associated with the Father, that introduces the reciprocal relation of one to the other; and thus we distinguish between the Persons. But, since the peculiar properties of the Persons produce a certain order, so that the original cause is in the Father, whenever the Father and the Son or Spirit are mentioned together, the name of God is peculiarly ascribed to the Father: by this method the unity of the essence is preserved, and the order is retained; which, however, derogates nothing from the Deity of the Son and Spirit. And indeed, as we have already seen that the Apostles assert him to be the Son of God, whom Moses and the Prophets have represented as Jehovah, it is always necessary to recur to the unity of the essence. Wherefore it would be a detestable sacrilege for us to call the Son another God different from the Father; because the simple name of God admits of no relation; nor can God, with respect to himself, be denominated either the one or the other. Now, that the name "Jehovah," in an indefinite sense, is applicable to Christ, appears even from the words of Paul: "for this thing I besought the Lord thrice;" because, after relating the answer of Christ, "My grace is sufficient for thee," he immediately subjoins, "That the power of Christ may rest upon me." For it is certain that the word "Lord" is there used for "Jehovah;" and to restrict it to the person of the Mediator, would be frivolous and puerile, since it is an absolute declaration, containing no comparison between the Son and the Father. And we know that the Apostles, following the custom of the Greek translators, invariably use the word Κυριος, (Lord,) instead of Jehovah. And, not to seek far for an example of this, Paul prayed to the Lord in no other sense than is intended in a passage of Joel, cited by Peter: "Whosoever shall call on the name of the Lord shall be saved." But for the peculiar ascription of this name to the Son, another reason will be given in its proper place; suffice it at present to observe that, when Paul had prayed to God absolutely, he immediately subjoins the name of Christ. Thus also the whole Deity is by Christ himself denominated "a Spirit." For nothing opposes the spirituality of the whole Divine essence, in which are comprehended the Father, the Son, and the Spirit; which is plain from the Scripture. For as we there find God denominated a Spirit, so we find also the Holy Spirit, forasmuch as he is an hypostasis of the whole essence, represented both as the Spirit of God, and as proceeding from God.

XXI. But since Satan, in order to subvert the very foundations of our faith, has always been exciting great contentions concerning the Divine essence of the Son and Spirit, and the distinction of the Persons; and in almost all ages has instigated impious spirits to vex the orthodox teachers on this account; and is also endeavouring, in the present day, with the old embers, to kindle a new flame; it becomes necessary here to refute the perverse and fanciful notions which some persons have imbibed. Hitherto it has been our principal design to instruct the docile, and not to combat the obstinate and contentious: but now, having calmly explained and proved the truth, we must vindicate it from all the cavils of the wicked; although I shall make it my principal study, that those who readily and implicitly attend to the Divine word, may have stable ground on which they may confidently rest. On this, indeed, if on any of the secret mysteries of the Scripture, we ought to philosophize with great sobriety and moderation; and also with extreme caution, lest either our ideas or our language should proceed beyond the limits of the Divine word. For how can the infinite essence of God be defined by the narrow capacity of the human mind, which could never yet certainly determine the nature of the body of the sun, though the object of our daily contemplation? How can the human mind, by its own efforts, penetrate into an examination of the essence of God, when it is totally ignorant of its own? Wherefore let us freely leave to God the knowledge of himself. For "he alone," as Hilary says, "is a competent witness for himself, being only known by himself." And we shall certainly leave it to him, if our conceptions of him correspond to the manifestations which he has given us of himself, and our inquiries concerning him are confined to his word. There are extant on this argument five homilies of Chrysostom against the Anomœi; which, however, were not sufficient to restrain the presumptuous garrulity of those sophists. For they discovered no greater modesty in this instance than in every other. The very unhappy consequences of this temerity should warn us to study this question with more docility than subtlety, and not allow ourselves to investigate God any where but in his sacred word, or to form any ideas of him but such as are agreeable to his word, or to speak any thing concerning him but what is derived from the same word. But if the distinction of Father, Son, and Spirit, in the one Deity, as it is not easy to be comprehended, occasions some understandings more labour and trouble than is desirable, let them remember that the mind of man, when it indulges its curiosity, enters into a labyrinth; and let them submit to be guided by the heavenly oracles, however they may not comprehend the height of this mystery.

XXII. To compose a catalogue of the errors, by which the purity of the faith has been attacked on this point of doctrine, would be too prolix and tedious, without being profitable; and most of the heretics so strenuously exerted themselves to effect the total extinction of the Divine glory by their gross reveries, that they thought it sufficient to unsettle and disturb the inexperienced. From a few men there soon arose numerous sects, of whom some would divide the Divine essence, and others would confound the distinction which subsists between the Persons. But if we maintain, what has already been sufficiently demonstrated from the Scripture, that the essence of the one God, which pertains to the Father, to the Son, and to the Spirit, is simple and undivided, and, on the other hand, that the Father is, by some property, distinguished from the Son, and likewise the Son from the Spirit, the gate will be shut, not only against Arius and Sabellius, but also against all the other ancient heresiarchs. But since our own times have witnessed some madmen, as Servetus and his followers, who have involved every thing in new subtleties, a brief exposure of their fallacies will not be unuseful. The word *Trinity* was so odious and even detestable to Servetus, that he asserted all Trinitarians, as he called them, to be Atheists. I omit his impertinent and scurrilous language, but this was the substance of his speculations: That it is representing God as consisting of three parts, when three Persons are said to subsist in his essence, and that this triad is merely imaginary, being repugnant to the Divine unity. At the same time, he maintained the Persons to be certain external ideas, which have no real subsistence in the Divine essence, but give us a figurative representation of God, under this or the other form; and that in the beginning there was no distinction in God, because the Word was once the same as the Spirit; but that, after Christ appeared God of God, there emanated from him another God, even the Spirit. Though he sometimes glosses over his impertinencies with allegories, as when he says, that the eternal Word of God was the Spirit of Christ with God, and the reflection of his image, and that the Spirit was a shadow of the Deity, yet he afterwards destroys the Deity of both, asserting that, according to the mode of dispensation, there is a part of God in both the Son and the Spirit; just as the same Spirit, substantially diffused in us, and even in wood and stones, is a portion of the Deity. What he broached concerning the Person of the Mediator, we shall examine in the proper place. But this monstrous fiction, that a Divine Person is nothing but a visible appearance of the glory of God, will not need a prolix refutation. For when John pronounces that the Word (Λογος) was God before the creation of the world, he sufficiently discriminates him from an ideal form. But if then also, and from the remotest eternity, that Word (Λογος) who was God, was with the Father, and possessed his own glory with the Father, he certainly could not be an external or figurative splendour; but it necessarily follows, that he was a real hypostasis, subsisting in God himself. But although no mention is made of the Spirit, but in the history of the creation of the world, yet he is there introduced, not as a shadow, but as the essential power of God, since Moses relates that the chaotic mass was supported by him. It then appeared, therefore, that the eternal Spirit had always existed in the Deity, since he cherished and sustained the confused matter of the heaven and earth, till it attained a state of beauty and order. He certainly could not then be an image or representation of God, according to the dreams of Servetus. But in other places he is constrained to make a fuller disclosure of his impiety, saying that God, in his eternal reason, decreeing for himself a visible Son, has visibly exhibited himself in this manner; for if this be true, there is no other Divinity left to Christ, than as he has been appointed a Son by an eternal decree of God. Besides, he so transforms those phantasms, which he substitutes instead of the hypostases, that he hesitates not to imagine new accidents or properties in God. But the most execrable blasphemy of all is, his promiscuous confusion of the Son of God and the Spirit with all the creatures. For he asserts that in the Divine essence there are parts and divisions, every portion of which is God; and especially that the souls of the faithful are coëternal and consubstantial with God; though in another place he assigns substantial Deity, not only to the human soul, but to all created things.

XXIII. From the same corrupt source has proceeded another heresy, equally monstrous. For some worthless men, to escape the odium and disgrace which attended the impious tenets of Servetus, have confessed, indeed, that there are three Persons, but with this explanation, that the Father, who alone is truly and properly God, hath created the Son and Spirit, and transfused his Deity into them. Nor do they refrain from this dreadful manner of expressing themselves, that the Father is distinguished from the Son and Spirit, as being the sole possessor of the Divine essence. Their first plea in support of this notion is, that Christ is commonly called the Son of God; whence they conclude that no other is properly God but the Father. But they observe not, that although the name of God is common also to the Son, yet that it is sometimes ascribed to the Father (κατ' ἐξοχην) by way of eminence, because he is the fountain and original of the Deity; and this in order to denote the simple unity of the essence. They object, that if he is truly the Son of God, it is absurd to account him the Son of a Person. I reply, that both are true; that he is the Son of God, because he is the Word begotten of the Father before time began, for we are not yet speaking of the Person of the Mediator; and to be explicit, we must notice the Person, that the name of God may not be understood absolutely, but for the Father; for if we acknowledge no other to be God than the Father, it will be a manifest degradation of the dignity of the Son. Whenever mention is made of the Deity, therefore, there must no opposition be admitted between the Father and the Son, as though the name of the true God belonged exclusively to the Father. For surely the God who appeared to Isaiah, was the only true God; whom, nevertheless, John affirms to have been Christ. He likewise, who by the mouth of Isaiah declared that he was to be a rock of offence to the Jews, was the only true God; whom Paul pronounces to have been Christ. He who proclaims by Isaiah, "As I live, every knee shall bow to me," is the only true God; but Paul applies the same to Christ. To the same purpose are the testimonies recited by the Apostle—"Thou, Lord, hast laid the foundation of the earth and the heavens;" and "Let all the angels of God worship him." These ascriptions belong only to the one true God; whereas he contends that they are properly applied to Christ. Nor is there any force in that cavil, that what is proper to God is transferred to Christ, because he is the brightness of his glory. For, since the name Jehovah is used in each of these passages, it follows that in respect of his Deity he is self-existent. For, if he is Jehovah, he cannot be denied to be the same God, who in another place proclaims by Isaiah, "I am the first and I am the last; and beside me there is no God." That passage in Jeremiah also deserves our attention—"The gods that have not made the heavens and the earth, even they shall perish from the earth, and from under these heavens;" whilst, on the contrary, it must be acknowledged, that the Deity of the Son of God is frequently proved by Isaiah from the creation of the world. But how shall the Creator, who gives existence to all, not be self-existent, but derive his essence from another? For whoever asserts that the Son owes his essence to the Father, denies him to be self-existent. But this is contradicted by the Holy Spirit, who gives him the name of Jehovah. Now, if we admit the whole essence to be solely in the Father, either it will be divisible, or it will be taken away from the Son; and so, being despoiled of his essence, he will be only a titular god. The Divine essence, according to these triflers, belongs solely to the Father, inasmuch as he alone possesses it, and is the author of the essence of the Son. Thus the Divinity of the Son will be a kind of emanation from the essence of God, or a derivation of a part from the whole. Now, they must of necessity concede, from their own premises, that the Spirit is the Spirit of the Father only; because if he be a derivation from the original essence, which belongs exclusively to the Father, he cannot be accounted the Spirit of the Son; which is refuted by the testimony of Paul, where he makes him common to Christ and the Father. Besides, if the Person of the Father be expunged from the Trinity, wherein will he differ from the Son and Spirit, but in being himself the sole Deity? They confess that Christ is God, and yet differs from the Father. Some distinctive character is necessary, also, to discriminate the Father from the Son. They who place this in the essence, manifestly destroy the true Deity of Christ, which cannot exist independently of the essence, that is, of the entire essence. The Father certainly cannot differ from the Son, unless he have something peculiar to himself, which is not common to the Son. What will they find, by which to distinguish him? If the difference be in the essence, let them tell us whether he has communicated the same to the Son. But this could not be done partially; for it would be an abomination to fabricate a demigod. Besides, this would miserably dismember the Divine essence. The necessary conclusion then is, that it is entirely and perfectly common to the Father and the Son. And if this be true, there cannot, in respect of the essence, be any difference between them. If it be objected that the Father, notwithstanding this communication of his essence, remains the only God with whom the essence continues, then Christ must be a figurative god, a god in appearance and name only, not in reality; because nothing is more proper to God than to be, according to that declaration, "I AM hath sent me unto you."

XXIV. We might readily prove from many passages the falsehood of their assumption, that, whenever the name of God is mentioned absolutely in the Scripture, it means only the Father. And in those places which they cite in their own defence, they shamefully betray their ignorance, since the Son is there added; from which it appears, that the name of God is used in a relative sense, and therefore is particularly restricted to the Person of the Father. Their objection, that, unless the Father alone were the true God, he would himself be his own Father, is answered in a word. For there is no absurdity in the name of God, for the sake of dignity and order, being peculiarly given to him, who not only hath begotten of himself his own wisdom, but is also the God of the Mediator, of which I shall treat more at large in its proper place. For since Christ was manifested in the flesh, he is called the Son of God, not only as he was the eternal Word begotten of the Father before time began, but because he assumed the person and office of a Mediator, to unite us to God. And since they so presumptuously exclude the Son from Divine honours, I would wish to be informed, when he declares that there is none good but the one God, whether he deprives himself of all goodness. I speak not of his human nature, lest they should object, that, whatever goodness it had, it was gratuitously conferred on it. I demand whether the eternal Word of God be good or not. If they answer in the negative, they are sufficiently convicted of impiety; and if in the affirmative, they cut the throat of their own system. But though, at the first glance, Christ seems to deny himself the appellation of good, he furnishes, notwithstanding, a further confirmation of our opinion. For, as that is a title which peculiarly belongs to the one God, forasmuch as he had been saluted as good, merely according to a common custom, by his rejection of false honour, he suggested that the goodness which he possessed was Divine. I demand, also, when Paul affirms that God alone is immortal, wise, and true, whether he thereby degrades Christ to the rank of those who are mortal, unwise, and false. Shall not he then be immortal who from the beginning was life itself, and the giver of immortality to angels? Shall not he be wise who is the eternal Wisdom of God? Shall not he be true who is truth itself? I demand further, whether they think that Christ ought to be worshipped. For, if he justly claims this as his right, that every knee should bow before him, it follows that he is that God, who, in the law, prohibited the worship of any one but himself. If they will have this passage in Isaiah, "I am, and there is no God besides me," to be understood solely of the Father, I retort this testimony on themselves; since we see that whatever belongs to God is attributed to Christ. Nor is there any room for their cavil, that Christ was exalted in the humanity in which he had been abased; and that, with regard to his humanity, all power was given to him in heaven and in earth; because, although the regal and judicial majesty extends to the whole Person of the Mediator, yet, had he not been God manifested in the flesh, he could not have been exalted to such an eminence, without God being in opposition to himself. And Paul excellently determines this controversy, by informing us that he was equal with God, before he abased himself under the form of a servant. Now, how could this equality subsist, unless he had been that God whose name is JAH and JEHOVAH, who rides on the cherubim, whose kingdom is universal and everlasting? No clamour of theirs can deprive Christ of another declaration of Isaiah: "Lo, this is our God, we have waited for him;" since in these words he describes the advent of God the Redeemer, not only for the deliverance of the people from exile in Babylon, but also for the complete restoration of the church. Nor do they gain any thing by another cavil, that Christ was God in his Father. For although we confess, in point of order and degree, that the Father is the fountain of the Deity, yet we pronounce it a detestable figment, that the essence belongs exclusively to the Father, as though he were the author of the Deity of the Son; because, on this supposition, either the essence would be divided, or Christ would be only a titular and imaginary god. If they admit that the Son is God, but inferior to the Father, then in him the essence must be begotten and created, which in the Father is unbegotten and uncreated. I know that some scorners ridicule our concluding a distinction of Persons from the words of Moses, where he introduces God thus speaking: "Let us make man in our image." Yet pious readers perceive how frigidly and foolishly Moses would have introduced this conference, if in one God there had not subsisted a plurality of Persons. Now, it is certain that they whom the Father addressed, were uncreated; but there is nothing uncreated, except the one God himself. Now, therefore, unless they grant that the power to create, and the authority to command, were common to the Father, the Son, and the Spirit, it will follow, that God did not speak thus within himself, but directed his conversation to some exterior agents. Lastly, one place will easily remove their two objections at once. For when Christ himself declares, that God is a Spirit, it would be unreasonable to restrict this solely to the Father, as though the Word were not also of a spiritual nature. But if the name of Spirit is equally as applicable to the Son as to the Father, I conclude that the Son is comprehended under the indefinite name of God. Yet he immediately subjoins, that none are approved worshippers of the Father, but those who worship him in spirit and in truth. Whence follows another consequence, that, because Christ performs the office of a Teacher, in a station of inferiority, he ascribes the name of God to the Father, not to destroy his own Deity, but by degrees to raise us to the knowledge of it.

XXV. But they deceive themselves in dreaming of three separate individuals, each of them possessing a part of the Divine essence. We teach, according to the Scriptures, that there is essentially but one God; and, therefore, that the essence of both the Son and the Spirit is unbegotten. But since the Father is first in order, and hath of himself begotten his wisdom, therefore, as has before been observed, he is justly esteemed the original and fountain of the whole Divinity. Thus God, indefinitely, is unbegotten; and the Father also is unbegotten with regard to his Person. They even foolishly suppose, that our opinion implies a quaternity; whereas they are guilty of falsehood and calumny, in ascribing to us a figment of their own; as though we pretended that the three Persons are as so many streams proceeding from one essence, when it is evident, from our writings, that we separate not the Persons from the essence, but, though they subsist in it, make a distinction between them. If the persons were separated from the essence, there would perhaps be some probability in their argument; but then there would be a trinity of Gods, not a trinity of persons contained in one God. This solves their frivolous question, whether the essence concurs to the formation of the Trinity; as though we imagined three Gods to descend from it. Their objection, that then the Trinity would be without God, is equally impertinent. Because, though it concurs not to the distinction as a part or member, yet the Persons are not independent of it, nor separate from it; for the Father, unless he were God, could not be the Father; and the Son is the Son only as he is God. Therefore we say, that the Deity is absolutely self-existent; whence we confess, also, that the Son, as God, independently of the consideration of Person, is self-existent; but as the Son, we say, that he is of the Father. Thus his essence is unoriginated; but the origin of his Person is God himself. And, indeed, the orthodox writers, who have written on the Trinity, have referred this name only to the Persons; since to comprehend the essence in that distinction, were not only an absurd error, but a most gross impiety. For it is evident that those who maintain that the Trinity consists in a union of the Essence, the Son, and the Spirit, annihilate the essence of the Son and of the Spirit; otherwise the parts would be destroyed by being confounded together; which is a fault in every distinction. Finally, if the words *Father* and *God* were synonymous—if the Father were the author of the Deity—nothing would be left in the Son but a mere shadow; nor would the Trinity be any other than a conjunction of the one God with two created things.

XXVI. Their objection, that Christ, if he be properly God, is not rightly called the Son of God, has already been answered; for when a comparison is made between one Person and another, the word *God* is not used indefinitely, but is restricted to the Father, as being the fountain of the Deity, not with regard to the essence, as fanatics falsely pretend, but in respect of order. This is the sense in which we ought to understand that declaration of Christ to his Father: "This is life eternal, that they might know thee, the only true God, and Jesus Christ, whom thou hast sent." For, speaking in the capacity of Mediator, he holds an intermediate station between God and men; yet without any diminution of his majesty. For, although he abased himself, yet he lost not his glory with the Father, which was hidden from the world. Thus the Apostle to the Hebrews, though he acknowledges that Christ was made for a short time inferior to the angels, yet, nevertheless, hesitates not to assert, that he is the eternal God, who laid the foundation of the earth. We must remember, therefore, that whenever Christ, in the capacity of Mediator, addresses the Father, he comprehends, under the name of God, the Divinity which belongs also to himself. Thus, when he said to his Apostles, "I go unto the Father, for my Father is greater than I," he attributes not to himself a secondary Divinity, as if he were inferior to the Father with respect to the eternal essence, but because, having obtained the glory of heaven, he gathers together the faithful to a participation of it with him; he represents the Father to be in a station superior to himself, just as the illustrious perfection of the splendour which appears in heaven excels that degree of glory which was visible in him during his incarnate state. For the same reason, Paul says, in another place, that Christ "shall deliver up the kingdom to God, even the Father, that God may be all in all." Nothing would be more absurd than to deny perpetual duration to the Deity of Christ. Now, if he will never cease to be the Son of God, but will remain for ever the same as he has been from the beginning, it follows, that by the name *Father* is intended the one sole Divine essence, which is common to them both. And it is certain that Christ descended to us, in order that, exalting us to the Father, he might at the same time exalt us to himself also, as being one with the Father. It is therefore neither lawful nor right to restrict the name of God exclusively to the Father, and to deny it to the Son. For even on this very account John asserts him to be the true God, that no one might suppose, that he possessed only a secondary degree of Deity, inferior to the Father. And I wonder what can be the meaning of these fabricators of new gods, when, after confessing that Christ is the true

God, they immediately exclude him from the Deity of the Father; as though there could be any true God but one alone, or as though a transfused Divinity were any thing but a novel fiction.

XXVII. Their accumulation of numerous passages from Irenæus, where he asserts the Father of Christ to be the only and eternal God of Israel, is a proof either of shameful ignorance, or of consummate wickedness. For they ought to have considered, that that holy man was then engaged in a controversy with some madmen, who denied that the Father of Christ was the same God that has spoken by Moses and the Prophets, but maintained that he was I know not what sort of phantasm, produced from the corruption of the world. His only object, therefore, is to show that no other God is revealed in the Scripture than the Father of Christ, and that it is impious to imagine any other; and therefore we need not wonder at his frequently concluding, that there never was any other God of Israel than he who was preached by Christ and his Apostles. So, now, on the other hand, when a different error is to be opposed, we shall truly assert, that the God who appeared formerly to the patriarchs, was no other than Christ. If it be objected that it was the Father, we are prepared to reply, that, while we contend for the Divinity of the Son, we by no means reject that of the Father. If the reader attends to this design of Irenæus, all contention will cease. Moreover, the whole controversy is easily decided by the sixth chapter of the third book, where the good man insists on this one point: That he who is absolutely and indefinitely called God in the Scripture, is the only true God; but that the name of God is given absolutely to Christ. Let us remember that the point at issue, as appears from the whole treatise, and particularly from the forty-sixth chapter of the second book, was this: That the appellation of Father is not given in an enigmatical and parabolical sense to one who is not truly God. Besides, in another place he contends, that the Son is called God, as well as the Father, by the Prophets and Apostles. He afterwards states how Christ, who is Lord, and King, and God, and Judge of all, received power from him who is God of all; and that is with relation to the subjection in which he was humbled even to the death of the cross. And a little after he affirms, that the Son is the Creator of heaven and earth, who gave the law by the hand of Moses, and appeared to the patriarchs. Now, if any one pretends that Irenæus acknowledges the Father alone as the God of Israel, I shall reply, as is clearly maintained by the same writer, that Christ is one and the same; as also he applies to him the prophecy of Habakkuk: "God shall come from the south." To the same purpose is what we find in the ninth chapter of the fourth book: "Therefore Christ himself is, with the Father, the God of the living." And in the twelfth chapter of the same book he states, that Abraham believed in God, inasmuch as Christ is the Creator of heaven and earth, and the only God.

XXVIII. Their pretensions to the sanction of Tertullian are equally unfounded, for, notwithstanding the occasional harshness and obscurity of his mode of expression, yet he unequivocally teaches the substance of the doctrine which we are defending; that is, that whereas there is one God, yet by dispensation or economy there is his Word; that there is but one God in the unity of the substance, but that the unity, by a mysterious dispensation, is disposed into a trinity; that there are three, not in condition, but in degree; not in substance, but in form; not in power, but in order. He says, indeed, that he maintains the Son to be second to the Father; but he applies this only to the distinction of the Persons. He says somewhere, that the Son is visible; but after having stated arguments on both sides, he concludes that, as the Word, he is invisible. Lastly, his assertion that the Father is designated by his Person, proves him to be at the greatest distance from the notion which we are refuting. And though he acknowledges no other God than the Father, yet the explanations which he gives in the immediate context show that he speaks not to the exclusion of the Son, when he denies the existence of any other God than the Father; and that therefore the unity of Divine government is not violated by the distinction of persons. And from the nature and design of his argument it is easy to gather the meaning of his words. For he contends, in opposition to Praxeas, that although God is distinguished into three Persons, yet neither is there a plurality of gods, nor is the unity divided. And because, according to the erroneous notion of Praxeas, Christ could not be God, without being the Father, therefore Tertullian bestows so much labour upon the distinction. His calling the Word and Spirit a portion of the whole, though a harsh expression, yet is excusable; since it has no reference to the substance, but only denotes the disposition and economy, which belongs solely to the Persons, according to the testimony of Tertullian himself. Hence also that question, "How many Persons suppose you that there are, O most perverse Praxeas, but as many as there are names?" So, a little after, "that they may believe the Father and the Son, both in their names and Persons." These arguments, I conceive, will suffice to refute the impudence of those who make use of the authority of Tertullian in order to deceive the minds of the simple.

XXIX. And certainly, whoever will diligently compare the writings of the fathers, will find in Irenæus nothing different from what was advanced by others who succeeded him. Justin Martyr is one of the most ancient; and he agrees with us in every point. They may object that the Father of Christ is denominated the one God by him as well as by the rest. The same is asserted also by Hilary, and even in harsher terms: he says, that eternity is in the Father; but does this imply a denial of the Divine essence to the Son? On the contrary, he had no other design than to maintain the same faith which we hold. Nevertheless, they are not ashamed to cull out mutilated passages, in order to induce a belief that he patronized their error. If they wish any authority to be attached to their quotation of Ignatius, let them prove that the Apostles delivered any law concerning Lent, and similar corruptions; for nothing can be more absurd than the impertinencies which have been published under the name of Ignatius. Wherefore their impudence is more intolerable, who disguise themselves under such false colours for the purpose of deception. Moreover, the consent of antiquity manifestly appears from this circumstance, that in the Nicene Council, Arius never dared to defend himself by the authority of any approved writer; and not one of the Greek or Latin fathers, who were there united against him, excused himself as at all dissenting from his predecessors. With regard to Augustine, who experienced great hostility from these disturbers, his diligent examination of all the writings of the earlier fathers, and his respectful attention to them, need not be mentioned. If he differs from them in the smallest particulars, he assigns the reasons which oblige him to dissent from them. On this argument also, if he finds any thing ambiguous or obscure in others, he never conceals it. Yet he takes it for granted, that the doctrine which those men oppose has been received without controversy from the remotest antiquity; and yet that he was not uninformed of what others had taught before him, appears even from one word in the first book of his Treatise on the Christian Doctrine, where he says, that unity is in the Father. Will they pretend that he had then forgotten himself? But he elsewhere vindicates himself from this calumny, where he calls the Father the fountain of the whole Deity, because he is from no other; wisely considering that the name of God is especially ascribed to the Father, because, unless the original be from him, it is impossible to conceive of the simple unity of the Deity. These observations, I hope, will be approved by the pious reader, as sufficient to refute all the calumnies, with which Satan has hitherto laboured to pervert or obscure the purity of this doctrine. Finally, I trust that the whole substance of this doctrine has been faithfully stated and explained, provided my readers set bounds to their curiosity, and are not unreasonably fond of tedious and intricate controversies. For I have not the least expectation of giving satisfaction to those who are pleased with an intemperance of speculation. I am sure I have used no artifice in the omission of any thing, from a supposition that it would make against me. But, studying the edification of the Church, I have thought it better not to touch upon many things, which would be unnecessarily burdensome to the reader, without yielding him any profit. For to what purpose is it to dispute, whether the Father be always begetting? For it is foolish to imagine a continual act of generation, since it is evident that three Persons have subsisted in God from all eternity.

5.

God's Preservation and Support of the World by His Power, and His Government of Every Part of It by His Providence.

To represent God as a Creator only for a moment, who entirely finished all his work at once, were frigid and jejune; and in this it behoves us specially to differ from the heathen, that the presence of the Divine power may appear to us no less in the perpetual state of the world than in its first origin. For although the minds even of impious men, by the mere contemplation of earth and heaven, are constrained to rise to the Creator, yet faith has a way peculiar to itself to assign to God the whole praise of creation. To which purpose is that assertion of an Apostle before cited, that it is only "through faith that we understand the worlds were framed by the word of God;" because, unless we proceed to his providence, we have no correct conception of the meaning of this article, "that God is the Creator;" however we may appear to comprehend it in our minds, and to confess it with our tongues. The carnal sense, when it has once viewed the power of God in the creation, stops there; and when it proceeds the furthest, it only examines and considers the wisdom, and power, and goodness, of the Author in producing such a work, which spontaneously present themselves to the view even of those who are unwilling to observe them. In the next place, it conceives of some general operation of God in preserving and governing it, on which the power of motion depends. Lastly, it supposes that the vigour originally infused by God into all things is sufficient for their sustentation. But faith ought to penetrate further. When it has learned that he is the Creator of all things, it should immediately conclude that he is also their perpetual governor and preserver; and that not by a certain universal motion, actuating the whole machine of the world, and all its respective parts, but by a particular providence sustaining, nourishing, and providing for everything which he has made. Thus David, having briefly premised that the world was made by God, immediately descends to the continual course of his providence: "By the word of the Lord were the heavens made; and all the host of them by the breath of his mouth." He afterwards adds, "The Lord beholdeth all the sons of men;" and subjoins more to the same purpose. For though all men argue not so skilfully, yet, since it would not be credible that God was concerned about human affairs, if he were not the Maker of the world, and no one seriously believes that the world was made by God, who is not persuaded that he takes care of his own works, it is not without reason that David conducts us by a most excellent series from one to the other. In general, indeed, both philosophers teach, and the minds of men conceive, that all the parts of the world are quickened by the secret inspiration of God. But they go not so far as David, who is followed by all the pious, when he says, "These all wait upon thee; that thou mayest give them their meat in due season. That thou givest them, they gather; thou openest thine hand, they are filled with good. Thou hidest thy face, they are troubled; thou takest away their breath, they die, and return to their dust. Thou sendest forth thy Spirit, they are created; and thou renewest the face of the earth." Though they subscribe to the assertion of Paul, that in God "we live, and move, and have our being," yet they are very far from a serious sense of his favour, celebrated by the Apostle; because they have no apprehension of the special care of

God, from which alone his paternal favour is known.

II. For the clearer manifestation of this difference, it must be observed that the providence of God, as it is taught in Scripture, is opposed to fortune and fortuitous accidents. Now, since it has been the common persuasion in all ages, and is also in the present day almost the universal opinion, that all things happen fortuitously, it is certain that every correct sentiment concerning providence is not only obscured, but almost buried in oblivion by this erroneous notion. If any one falls into the hands of robbers, or meets with wild beasts; if by a sudden storm he is shipwrecked on the ocean; if he is killed by the fall of a house or a tree; if another, wandering through deserts, finds relief for his penury, or, after having been tossed about by the waves, reaches the port, and escapes, as it were, but a hair's-breadth from death,—carnal reason will ascribe all these occurrences, both prosperous and adverse, to fortune. But whoever has been taught from the mouth of Christ, that the hairs of his head are all numbered, will seek further for a cause, and conclude that all events are governed by the secret counsel of God. And respecting things inanimate, it must be admitted, that, though they are all naturally endued with their peculiar properties, yet they exert not their power, any further than as they are directed by the present hand of God. They are, therefore, no other than instruments into which God infuses as much efficacy as he pleases, bending and turning them to any actions, according to his will. There is no power among all the creatures more wonderful or illustrious, than that of the sun. For, besides his illumination of the whole world by his splendour, how astonishing it is that he cherishes and enlivens all animals with his heat; with his rays inspires fecundity into the earth; from the seeds, genially warmed in her bosom, produces a green herbage, which, being supported by fresh nourishment, he increases and strengthens till it rises into stalks; feeds them with perpetual exhalations, till they grow into blossoms, and from blossoms to fruit, which he then by his influences brings to maturity; that trees, likewise, and vines, by his genial warmth, first put forth leaves, then blossoms, and from the blossoms produce their fruit! But the Lord, to reserve the praise of all these things entirely to himself, was pleased that the light should exist, and the earth abound in every kind of herbs and fruits, before he created the sun. A pious man, therefore, will not make the sun either a principal or necessary cause of those things which existed before the creation of the sun, but only an instrument which God uses, because it is his pleasure so to do; whereas he would find no more difficulty in acting by himself without that luminary. Lastly, as we read that the sun remained in one situation for two days at the prayer of Joshua, and that his shadow made a retrograde motion of ten degrees for the sake of king Hezekiah, God has declared by these few miracles, that the daily rising and setting of the sun is not from a blind instinct of nature, but that he himself governs his course, to renew the memory of his paternal favour towards us. Nothing is more natural than the succession of spring to winter, of summer to spring, and of autumn to summer. But there is so great a diversity and inequality discovered in this series, that it is obvious that every year, month, and day, is governed by a new and particular providence of God.

III. And, indeed, God asserts his possession of omnipotence, and claims our acknowledgment of this attribute; not such as is imagined by sophists, vain, idle, and almost asleep, but vigilant, efficacious, operative, and engaged in continual action; not a mere general principle of confused motion, as if he should command a river to flow through the channels once made for it, but a power constantly exerted on every distinct and particular movement. For he is accounted omnipotent, not because he is able to act, yet sits down in idleness, or continues by a general instinct the order of nature originally appointed by him; but because he governs heaven and earth by his providence, and regulates all things in such a manner that nothing happens but according to his counsel. For when it is said in the Psalms, that he does whatsoever he pleases, it denotes his certain and deliberate will. For it would be quite insipid to expound the words of the Prophet in the philosophical manner, that God is the prime agent, because he is the principle and cause of all motion; whereas the faithful should rather encourage themselves in adversity with this consolation, that they suffer no affliction, but by the ordination and command of God, because they are under his hand. But if the government of God be thus extended to all his works, it is a puerile cavil to limit it to the influence and course of nature. And they not only defraud God of his glory, but themselves of a very useful doctrine, who confine the Divine providence within such narrow bounds, as though he permitted all things to proceed in an uncontrolled course, according to a perpetual law of nature; for nothing would exceed the misery of man, if he were exposed to all the motions of the heaven, air, earth, and waters. Besides, this notion would shamefully diminish the singular goodness of God towards every individual. David exclaims, that infants yet hanging on the breasts of their mothers are sufficiently eloquent to celebrate the glory of God; because, as soon as they are born, they find aliment prepared for them by his heavenly care. This, indeed, is generally true; yet it cannot escape the observation of our eyes and senses, being evidently proved by experience, that some mothers have breasts full and copious, but others almost dry; as it pleases God to provide more liberally for one, but more sparingly for another. But they who ascribe just praise to the Divine omnipotence, receive from this a double advantage. In the first place, he must have ample ability to bless them, who possesses heaven and earth, and whose will all the creatures regard so as to devote themselves to his service. And, secondly, they may securely repose in his protection, to whose will are subject all those evils which can be feared from any quarter; by whose power Satan is restrained, with all his furies, and all his machinations; on whose will depends all that is inimical to our safety; nor is there any thing else by which those immoderate and superstitious fears, which we frequently feel on the sight of dangers, can be corrected or appeased. We are superstitiously timid, I say, if, whenever creatures menace or terrify us, we are frightened, as though they had of themselves the power to hurt us, or could fortuitously injure us; or as if against their injuries God were unable to afford us sufficient aid. For example, the Prophet forbids the children of God to fear the stars and signs of heaven, as is the custom of unbelievers. He certainly condemns not every kind of fear. But when infidels transfer the government of the world from God to the stars, pretending that their happiness or misery depends on the decrees and presages of the stars, and not on the will of God, the consequence is, that their fear is withdrawn from him, whom alone they ought to regard, and is placed on stars and comets. Whoever, then, desires to avoid this infidelity, let him constantly remember, that in the creatures there is no erratic power, or action, or motion; but that they are so governed by the secret counsel of God, that nothing can happen but what is subject to his knowledge, and decreed by his will.

IV. First, then, let the readers know that what is called providence describes God, not as idly beholding from heaven the transactions which happen in the world, but as holding the helm of the universe, and regulating all events. Thus it belongs no less to his hands than to his eyes. When Abraham said to his son, "God will provide," he intended not only to assert his prescience of a future event, but to leave the care of a thing unknown to the will of him who frequently puts an end to circumstances of perplexity and confusion. Whence it follows, that providence consists in action; for it is ignorant trifling to talk of mere prescience. Not quite so gross is the error of those who attribute to God a government, as I have observed, of a confused and promiscuous kind; acknowledging that God revolves and impels the machine of the world, with all its parts, by a general motion, without peculiarly directing the action of each individual creature. Yet even this error is not to be tolerated. For they maintain that this providence, which they call universal, is no impediment either to all the creatures being actuated contingently, or to man turning himself hither or thither at the free choice of his own will. And they make the following partition between God and man; that God by his power inspires him with motions, enabling him to act according to the tendency of the nature with which he is endued; but that man governs his actions by his own voluntary choice. In short, they conceive, that the world, human affairs, and men themselves, are governed by the power of God, but not by his appointment. I speak not of the Epicureans, who have always infested the world, who dream of a god absorbed in sloth and inactivity; and of others no less erroneous, who formerly pretended that the dominion of God extended over the middle region of the air, but that he left inferior things to fortune; since the mute creatures themselves sufficiently exclaim against such evident stupidity. My present design is to refute that opinion, which has almost generally prevailed, which, conceding to God a sort of blind and uncertain motion, deprives him of the principal thing, which is his directing and disposing, by his incomprehensible wisdom, all things to their proper end; and thus, robbing God of the government of the world, it makes him the ruler of it in name only, and not in reality. For, pray, what is governing, but presiding in such a manner, as to rule, by fixed decrees, those over whom you preside? Yet I reject not altogether what they assert concerning universal providence, provided they, on their part admit that God governs the world, not merely because he preserves the order of nature fixed by himself, but because he exercises a peculiar care over every one of his works. It is true that all things are actuated by a secret instinct of nature, as though they obeyed the eternal command of God, and that what God has once appointed, appears to proceed from voluntary inclination in the creatures. And to this may be referred the declaration of Christ, that his Father and himself had always been working, even from the beginning; and the assertion of Paul, that "in him we live, and move, and have our being;" and also what is observed by the author of the Epistle to the Hebrews, with a design to prove the Divinity of Christ, that all things are sustained by the word of his power. But they act very improperly in concealing and obscuring, by this pretext, the doctrine of a particular providence, which is asserted in such plain and clear testimonies of Scripture, that it is surprising how any one could entertain a doubt concerning it. And, certainly, they who conceal it with this veil which I have mentioned, are obliged to correct themselves by adding, that many things happen through the peculiar care of God; but this they erroneously restrict to some particular acts. Wherefore we have to prove, that God attends to the government of particular events, and that they all proceed from his determinate counsel, in such a manner that there can be no such thing as fortuitous contingence.

V. If we grant that the principle of motion originates from God, but that all things are spontaneously or accidentally carried whither the bias of nature impels them, the mutual vicissitudes of day and night, of winter and summer, will be the work of God, inasmuch as he has distributed to each its respective parts, and prescribed to them a certain law; that is, this would be the case if with even tenor they always observed the same measure, days succeeding to nights, months to months, and years to years. But sometimes excessive heats and drought parch and burn the fruits of the earth; sometimes unseasonable rains injure the crops of corn, and sudden calamities are occasioned by showers of hail and storms: this will not be the work of God; unless, perhaps, as either clouds or serene weather, or cold or heat, derive their origin from the opposition of the stars and other natural causes. But this representation leaves no room for God to display or exercise his paternal favour, or his judgments. If they say that God is sufficiently beneficent to man, because he infuses into heaven and earth an ordinary power, by which they supply him with food, it is a very flimsy and profane notion; as though the fecundity of one year were not the singular benediction of God, and as though penury and famine were not his malediction and vengeance. But as it would be tedious to collect all the reasons for rejecting this error, let us be content with the authority of God himself. In the law and in the prophets he frequently declares, that whenever he moistens the earth with dew or with rain, he affords a testimony of his favour; and that, on the contrary, when, at his command, heaven becomes hard as iron, when the crops of corn are blasted and otherwise destroyed, and when showers of hail and storms molest the fields, he gives a proof of his certain and special vengeance. If we believe these things, it is certain that not a drop of rain falls but at the express command of God. David indeed praises the general providence of God, because "he giveth food to the young ravens which cry;" but when God himself threatens animals with famine, does he not plainly declare, that he feeds all living creatures, sometimes with a smaller allowance, sometimes with a larger, as he pleases? It is puerile, as I have already observed, to restrain this to particular acts; whereas Christ says, without any exception, that not a sparrow of the least value falls to the ground without the will of the Father. Certainly, if the flight of birds be directed by the unerring counsel of God, we must be constrained to confess with the Prophet, that, though "he dwelleth on high," yet "he humbleth himself to behold the things which are in heaven and in the earth."

VI. But as we know that the world was made chiefly for the sake of mankind, we must also observe this end in the government of it. The Prophet Jeremiah exclaims, "I know that the way of man is not in himself: it is not in man that walketh to direct his steps." And Solomon: "Man's goings are of the Lord: how can a man then understand his own way?" Now, let them say that man is actuated by God according to the bias of his nature, but that he directs that influence according to his own pleasure. If this could be asserted with truth, man would have the free choice of his own ways. That, perhaps, they will deny, because he can do nothing independently of the power of God. But since it is evident that both the Prophet and Solomon ascribe to God choice and appointment, as well as power, this by no means extricates them from the difficulty. But Solomon, in another place, beautifully reproves this temerity of men, who predetermine on an end for themselves, without regard to God, as though they were not led by his hand: "The preparation of the heart in man," says he, "and the answer of the tongue, is from the Lord." It is, indeed, a ridiculous madness for miserable men to resolve on undertaking any work independently of God, whilst they cannot even speak a word but what he chooses. Moreover, the Scripture, more fully to express that nothing is transacted in the world but according to his destination, shows that those things are subject to him which appear most fortuitous. For what would you be more ready to attribute to chance, than when a limb broken off from a tree kills a passing traveller? But very different is the decision of the Lord, who acknowledges that he has delivered him into the hand of the slayer. Who, likewise, does not leave lots to the blindness of fortune? Yet the Lord leaves them not, but claims the disposal of them himself. He teaches us that it is not by any power of their own that lots are cast into the lap and drawn out; but the only thing which could be ascribed to chance, he declares to belong to himself. To the same purpose is another passage from Solomon: "The poor and the deceitful man meet together: the Lord enlighteneth the eyes of them both." For although the poor and the rich are blended together in the world, yet, as their respective conditions are assigned to them by Divine appointment, he suggests that God, who enlightens all, is not blind, and thus exhorts the poor to patience; because those who are discontented with their lot, are endeavouring to shake off the burden imposed on them by God. Thus also another Prophet rebukes profane persons, who attribute it to human industry, or to fortune, that some men remain in obscurity, and others rise to honours: "Promotion cometh neither from the east, nor from the west, nor from the south. But God is the Judge; he putteth down one, and setteth up another." Since God cannot divest himself of the office of a judge, hence he reasons, that it is from the secret counsel of God, that some rise to promotion, and others remain in contempt.

VII. Moreover, particular events are in general proofs of the special providence of God. God raised in the desert a south wind, to convey to the people a large flock of birds. When he would have Jonah thrown into the sea, he sent forth a wind to raise a tempest. It will be said by them who suppose God not to hold the helm of the world, that this was a deviation from the common course of things. But the conclusion which I deduce from it is, that no wind ever rises or blows but by the special command of God. For otherwise it would not be true that he makes the winds his messengers, and a flame of fire his ministers, that he makes the clouds his chariot, and rides on the wings of the wind, unless he directed at his pleasure the course both of the clouds and of the winds, and displayed in them the singular presence of his power. Thus also we are elsewhere taught, that, whenever the sea is blown into a tempest by the winds, those commotions prove the special presence of God. "He commandeth and raiseth the stormy wind, which lifteth up the waves" of the sea. "Then he maketh the storm a calm, so that the waves thereof are still;" as in another place he proclaims, that he scourged the people with parching winds. Thus, whilst men are naturally endued with a power of generation, yet God will have it acknowledged as the effect of his special favour, that he leaves some without any posterity, and bestows children on others; for "the fruit of the womb is his reward." Therefore Jacob said to his wife, "Am I in God's stead, who hath withheld from thee the fruit of the womb?" But to conclude; there is nothing more common in nature, than for us to be nourished with bread. But the Spirit declares, not only that the produce of the earth is the special gift of God, but that men do not live by bread alone; because they are supported not by the abundance of their food, but by the secret benediction of God; as, on the contrary, he threatens that he will break "the stay of bread." Nor, indeed, could we otherwise seriously offer a prayer for daily bread, if God did not supply us with food from his fatherly hand. The Prophet, therefore, to convince the faithful that in feeding them God acts the part of an excellent father of a family, informs us, that he "giveth food to all flesh." Lastly, when we hear, on the one hand, that "the eyes of the Lord are upon the righteous, and his ears are open unto their cry," and, on the other, that "the face of the Lord is against them that do evil, to cut off the remembrance of them from the earth," we may be assured that all creatures, above and below, are ready for his service, that he may apply them to any use that he pleases. Hence we conclude, not only that there is a general providence of God over the creatures, to continue the order of nature, but that, by his wonderful counsel, they are all directed to some specific and proper end.

VIII. Those who wish to bring an odium on this doctrine, calumniate it as the same with the opinion of the Stoics concerning fate, with which Augustine also was formerly reproached. Though we are averse to all contentions about words, yet we admit not the term *fate*; both because it is of that novel and profane kind which Paul teaches us to avoid, and because they endeavour to load the truth of God with the odium attached to it. But that dogma is falsely and maliciously charged upon us. For we do not, with the Stoics, imagine a necessity arising from a perpetual concatenation and intricate series of causes, contained in nature; but we make God the Arbiter and Governor of all things, who, in his own wisdom, has, from the remotest eternity, decreed what he would do, and now, by his own power, executes what he has decreed. Whence we assert, that not only the heaven and the earth, and inanimate creatures, but also the deliberations and volitions of men, are so governed by his providence, as to be directed to the end appointed by it. What then? you will say; does nothing happen fortuitously or contingently? I answer, that it was truly observed by Basil the Great, that *fortune* and *chance* are words of the heathen, with the signification of which the minds of the pious ought not to be occupied. For if all success be the benediction of God, and calamity and adversity his malediction, there is no room left in human affairs for fortune or chance. And we should attend to this declaration of Augustine: "I am not pleased with myself," says he, "for having, in my treatises against the Academics, so frequently mentioned *fortune*, although I have not intended by that word any goddess, but a fortuitous occurrence of external things, either good or evil. Hence also such words, the use of which no religion prohibits, as *perhaps, perchance, peradventure*, which, nevertheless, must be entirely referred to the Divine providence. And on this I have not been silent, remarking that perhaps what is commonly termed *fortune* is regulated by a secret order, and that what we call *chance* is only that, with the reason and cause of which we are not acquainted. Thus, indeed, I have expressed myself; but I repent of having mentioned *fortune* in this manner, since I see that men are habituated to a very sinful custom: when they ought to say, 'This was the will of God,' they say, 'This was the will of Fortune.' " Finally, he every where maintains, that if any thing be left to fortune, the world revolves at random. And though he elsewhere decides, that all things are conducted partly by the free will of man, partly by the providence of God, yet he just after shows that men are subject to it and governed by it, assuming as a principle that nothing could be more absurd, than for any thing to happen independently of the ordination of God; because it would happen at random. By this reasoning he excludes also any contingence dependent on the human will; and immediately after more expressly asserts that we ought not to inquire for any cause of the will of God. But in what sense *permission* ought to be understood, whenever it is mentioned by him, will appear from one passage; where he proves that the will of God is the supreme and first cause of all things, because nothing happens but by his command or permission. He certainly does not suppose God to remain an idle spectator, determining to permit any thing; there is an intervention of actual volition, if I may be allowed the expression, which otherwise could never be considered as a cause.

IX. Yet, since the dulness of our minds is very much below the sublimity of the Divine providence, let us endeavour to assist them by a distinction. I say, then, that, notwithstanding the ordination of all things by the certain purpose and direction of God, yet to us they are fortuitous: not that we suppose fortune holds any dominion over the world and mankind, and whirls about all things at random, for such folly ought to be far from the breast of a Christian; but because the order, reason, end, and necessity of events are chiefly concealed in the purpose of God, and not comprehended by the mind of man, those things are in some measure fortuitous, which must certainly happen according to the Divine will. For they present no other appearance, whether they are considered in their own nature, or are estimated according to our knowledge and judgment. Let us suppose, for example, that a merchant, having entered a wood in the company of honest men, imprudently wanders from his companions, and, pursuing a wrong course, falls into the hands of robbers, and is murdered. His death was not only foreseen by God, but also decreed by him. For it is said, not that he has foreseen to what limits the life of every man would extend, but that he "hath appointed bounds which he cannot pass." Yet, as far as our minds are capable of comprehending, all these circumstances appear fortuitous. What opinion shall a Christian form on this case? He will consider all the circumstances of such a death as in their nature fortuitous; yet he will not doubt that the providence of God presided, and directed fortune to that end. The same reasoning will apply to future contingencies. All future things being uncertain to us, we hold them in suspense, as though they might happen either one way or another. Yet this remains a fixed principle in our hearts, that there will be no event which God has not ordained. In this sense the word *chance* is frequently repeated in the book of Ecclesiastes; because, on the first view, men penetrate not to the first cause, which lies deeply concealed. And yet the doctrine of the Scripture respecting the secret providence of God, has never been so far obliterated from the hearts of men, but that some sparks of it always shone in the darkness. Thus the Philistine sorcerers, though they fluctuated in uncertainty, ascribed adverse accidents partly to God, partly to fortune. "If the ark," say they, "goeth up by that way, we shall know that God hath done us this great evil; but if not, it was a chance that happened to us." They betrayed great folly, indeed, after having been deceived by divination, to have recourse to fortune; yet at the same time, we see them restrained, so that they cannot dare to suppose the affliction which had befallen them was fortuitous. But how God, by the reins of his providence, directs all events according to his own pleasure, will appear by an eminent example. At the very same instant of time when David had been overtaken in the wilderness of Maon, behold, the Philistines made an irruption into the land, and Saul was compelled to depart. If God, consulting the safety of his servant, laid this impediment in the way of Saul, then, surely, though the Philistines might have taken up arms suddenly, and contrary to human expectation, yet we will not say that this happened by chance; but what to us seems a contingency, faith will acknowledge to have been a secret impulse of God. It is not always, indeed, that there appears a similar reason; but it should be considered as indubitably certain, that all the revolutions visible in the world proceed from the secret exertion of the Divine power. What God decrees, must necessarily come to pass; yet it is not by absolute or natural necessity. We find a familiar example in respect to the bones of Christ. Since he possessed a body like ours, no reasonable man will deny that his bones were capable of being broken; yet that they should be broken was impossible. Hence, again, we perceive that the distinctions of relative and absolute necessity, as well as necessity of consequent and of consequence, were not without reason invented in the schools; since God made the bones of his Son capable of being broken, which, however, he had exempted from being actually broken, and thus prevented, by the necessity of his purpose, what might naturally have come to pass.

6.

The Proper Application of This Doctrine to Render It Useful to Us.

As the minds of men are prone to vain subtleties, there is the greatest danger that those who know not the right use of this doctrine will embarrass themselves with intricate perplexities. It will therefore be necessary to touch in a brief manner on the end and design of the Scripture doctrine of the Divine ordination of all things. And here let it be remarked, in the first place, that the providence of God is to be considered as well in regard to futurity, as in reference to that which is past; secondly, that it governs all things in such a manner as to operate sometimes by the intervention of means, sometimes without means, and sometimes in opposition to all means; lastly, that it tends to show the care of God for the whole human race, and especially his vigilance in the government of the Church, which he favours with more particular attention. It must also be observed, that, although the paternal favour and beneficence of God, or the severity of his justice, is frequently conspicuous in the whole course of his providence, yet sometimes the causes of events are concealed, so that a suspicion intrudes itself, that the revolutions of human affairs are conducted by the blind impetuosity of fortune; or the flesh solicits us to murmur, as though God amused himself with tossing men about like tennis-balls. It is true, indeed, if we were ready to learn with quiet and sober minds, that the final issue sufficiently proves the counsels of God to be directed by the best of reasons; that he designs either to teach his people the exercise of patience, or to correct their corrupt affections and subdue the licentiousness of their appetites, or to constrain them to the practice of self-denial, or to arouse them from their indolence; and, on the other hand, to abase the proud, to disappoint the cunning of the wicked, and to confound their machinations. Yet, however the causes may be concealed from us, or escape our observation, we must admit it as a certain truth, that they are hidden with him; and must therefore exclaim with David, "Many, O Lord my God, are thy wonderful works which thou hast done, and thy thoughts which are to us-ward: they cannot be reckoned up in order unto thee: if I would declare and speak of them, they are more than can be numbered." For, though our miseries ought always to remind us of our sins, that the punishment itself may urge us to repentance, yet we see that Christ ascribes more sovereignty to the secret purpose of the Father in afflicting men, than to require him to punish every individual according to his demerits. For concerning him who was born blind, he says, "Neither hath this man sinned, nor his parents; but that the works of God should be made manifest in him." For here sense murmurs, when calamity precedes the very birth, as though it were a detraction from the Divine clemency thus to afflict the innocent. But Christ declares that the glory of his Father is manifested in this instance, provided our eyes are clear to behold it. But we must proceed with modesty, cautious that we call not God to an account at our tribunal; but that we entertain such reverence for his secret judgments, as to esteem his will the most righteous cause of every thing that he does. When thick clouds obscure the heavens, and a violent tempest arises, because a gloomy mist is before our eyes, and thunder strikes our ears, and terror stupefies all our faculties, all things seem to us to be blended in confusion; yet during the whole time the heavens remain in the same quiet serenity. So it must be concluded, that while the turbulent state of the world deprives us of our judgment, God, by the pure light of his own righteousness and wisdom, regulates all those commotions in the most exact order, and directs them to their proper end. And certainly the madness of many in this respect is monstrous, who dare to arraign the works of God, to scrutinize his secret counsels, and even to pass a precipitate sentence on things unknown, with greater freedom than on the actions of mortal men. For what is more preposterous than towards our equals to observe such modesty, as rather to suspend our judgment than to incur the imputation of temerity, but impudently to insult the mysterious judgments of God, which we ought to hold in admiration and reverence?

II. None, therefore, will attain just and profitable views of the providence of God, but he who considers that he has to do with his Maker and the Creator of the world, and submits himself to fear and reverence with all becoming humility. Hence it happens that so many worthless characters in the present day virulently oppose this doctrine, because they will admit nothing to be lawful for God, but what agrees with the dictates of their own reason. They revile us with the utmost possible impudence, because, not content with the precepts of the law, which comprehend the will of God, we say that the world is governed also by his secret counsels; as though, indeed, what we assert were only an invention of our own brain, and the Holy Spirit did not every where plainly announce the same, and repeat it in innumerable forms of expression. But as they are restrained by some degree of shame from daring to discharge their blasphemies against heaven, in order to indulge their extravagance with greater freedom, they pretend that they are contending with us. But unless they admit, that whatever comes to pass in the world is governed by the incomprehensible counsel of God, let them answer, to what purpose is it said in the Scripture that his "judgments are a great deep"? For since Moses proclaims, that the will of God is not to be sought far off, in the clouds or in the deep, because it is familiarly explained in the law, it follows that there is another secret will, which is compared to a profound abyss; concerning which Paul also says, "O the depth of the riches both of the wisdom and knowledge of God; how unsearchable are his judgments, and his ways past finding out! For who hath known the mind of the Lord, or who hath been his counsellor?" It is true, that the law and the Gospel contain mysteries which far transcend our capacities; but since God illuminates the minds of his people with the spirit of understanding, to apprehend these mysteries which he has condescended to reveal in his word, there we have now no abyss, but a way in which we may safely walk, and a lamp for the direction of our feet, the light of life, and the school of certain and evident truth. But his admirable method of governing the world is justly called a "great deep," because, while it is concealed from our view, it ought to be the object of our profound adoration. Moses has beautifully expressed both in a few words. "The secret things," says he, "belong unto the Lord our God; but those things which are revealed belong unto us and to our children." We see how he enjoins us, not only to devote our attention to meditations on the law of God, but to look up with reverence to his mysterious providence. This sublime doctrine is declared in the book of Job, for the purpose of humbling our minds. For the author concludes a general view of the machine of the world, and a magnificent dissertation on the works of God, in these words: "Lo, these are parts of his ways; but how little a portion is heard of him!" For which reason, in another place he distinguishes between the wisdom which resides in God, and the method of attaining wisdom which he has prescribed to men. For, after discoursing concerning the secrets of nature, he says, that wisdom is known only to God, and "is hid from the eyes of all living." But a little after he subjoins, that it is published in order to be investigated, because it is said to men, "Behold the fear of the Lord, that is wisdom." To the same purpose is this observation of Augustine: "Because we know not all that God does concerning us by an excellent order we act according to the law in a good will only, but in other respects are actuated according to it; because his providence is an immutable law." Therefore, since God claims a power unknown to us of governing the world, let this be to us the law of sobriety and modesty, to acquiesce in his supreme dominion, to account his will the only rule of righteousness, and most righteous cause of all things. Not, indeed, that absolute will which is the subject of the declamation of sophists, impiously and profanely separating his justice from his power, but that providence which governs all things, from which originates nothing but what is right, although the reasons of it may be concealed from us.

III. Those who have learned this modesty, will neither murmur against God on account of past adversities, nor charge him with the guilt of their crimes, like Agamemnon, in Homer, who says, "The blame belongs not to me, but to Jupiter and Fate." Nor will they, as if hurried away by the Fates, under the influence of despair, put an end to their own lives, like the young man whom Plautus introduces as saying, "The condition of our affairs is inconstant; men are governed by the caprice of the Fates; I will betake myself to a precipice, and there destroy my life and every thing at once." Nor will they excuse their flagitious actions by ascribing them to God, after the example of another young man introduced by the same poet, who says, "God was the cause: I believe it was the Divine will. For had it not been so, I know it would not have happened." But they will rather search the Scripture, to learn what is pleasing to God, that by the guidance of the Spirit they may strive to attain it; and at the same time, being prepared to follow God whithersoever he calls them, they will exhibit proofs in their conduct that nothing is more useful than a knowledge of this doctrine. Some profane men foolishly raise such a tumult with their absurdities, as almost, according to a common expression, to confound heaven and earth together. They argue in this manner: If God has fixed the moment of our death, we cannot avoid it; therefore all caution against it will be but lost labour. One man dares not venture himself in a way which he hears is dangerous, lest he should be assassinated by robbers; another sends for physicians, and wearies himself with medicines, to preserve his life; another abstains from the grosser kinds of food, lest he should injure his valetudinary constitution; another dreads to inhabit a ruinous house; and men in general exert all their faculties in devising and executing methods by which they may attain the object of their desires. Now, either all these things are vain remedies employed to correct the will of God, or life and death, health and disease, peace and war, and other things which, according to their desires or aversions, men industriously study to obtain or to avoid, are not determined by his certain decree. Moreover they conclude, that the prayers of the faithful are not only superfluous, but perverse, which contain petitions that the Lord will provide for those things which he has already decreed from eternity. In short, they supersede all deliberations respecting futurity, as opposed to the providence of God, who, without consulting men, has decreed whatever he pleased. And what has already happened they impute to the Divine providence in such a manner as to overlook the person, who is known to have committed any particular act. Has an assassin murdered a worthy citizen? they say he has executed the counsel of God. Has any one been guilty of theft or fornication? because he has done what was foreseen and ordained by the Lord, he is the minister of his providence. Has a son, neglecting all remedies, carelessly waited the death of his father? it was impossible for him to resist God, who had decreed this event from eternity. Thus by these persons all crimes are denominated virtues, because they are subservient to the ordination of God.

IV. But in reference to future things, Solomon easily reconciles the deliberations of men with the providence of God. For as he ridicules the folly of those who presumptuously undertake any thing without the Lord, as though they were not subject to his government, so in another place he says, "A man's heart deviseth his way; but the Lord directeth his steps;" signifying that the eternal decrees of God form no impediment to our providing for ourselves, and disposing all our concerns in subservience to his will. The reason of this is manifest. For he who has fixed the limits of our life, has also intrusted us with the care of it; has furnished us with means and supplies for its preservation; has also made us provident of dangers; and, that they may not oppress us unawares, has furnished us with cautions and remedies. Now, it is evident what is our duty. If God has committed to us the preservation of our life, we should preserve it; if he offers supplies, we should use them; if he forewarns us of dangers, we should not rashly run into them; if he furnishes remedies, we ought not to neglect them. But it will be objected, no danger can hurt, unless it has been ordained that it shall hurt us, and then no remedies can avert it. But what if dangers are therefore not fatal, because God has assigned you remedies to repulse and overcome them? Examine whether your reasoning agrees with the order of the Divine providence. You conclude that it is unnecessary to guard against danger, because, if it be not fatal, we shall escape it without caution; but, on the contrary, the Lord enjoins you to use caution, because he intends it not to be fatal to you. These madmen overlook what is obvious to every observer—that the arts of deliberation and caution in men proceed from the inspiration of God, and that they subserve the designs of his providence in the preservation of their own lives; as, on the contrary, by neglect and slothfulness, they procure to themselves the evils which he has appointed for them. For how does it happen, that a prudent man, consulting his own welfare, averts from himself impending evils, and a fool is ruined by his inconsiderate temerity, unless folly and prudence are in both cases instruments of the Divine dispensation? Therefore it has pleased God to conceal from us all future events, that we may meet them as doubtful contingencies, and not cease to oppose to them the remedies with which we are provided, till they shall have been surmounted, or shall have overcome all our diligence. Therefore I have before suggested, that the providence of God ought not always to be contemplated abstractedly by itself, but in connection with the means which he employs.

V. The same persons inconsiderately and erroneously ascribe all past events to the absolute providence of God. For since all things which come to pass are dependent upon it, therefore, say they, neither thefts, nor adulteries, nor homicides, are perpetrated without the intervention of the Divine will. Why, therefore, they ask, shall a thief be punished for having pillaged him whom it has pleased the Lord to chastise with poverty? Why shall a homicide be punished for having slain him whose life the Lord had terminated? If all such characters are subservient to the Divine will, why shall they be punished? But I deny that they serve the will of God. For we cannot say, that he who is influenced by a wicked heart, acts in obedience to the commands of God, while he is only gratifying his own malignant passions. That man obeys God, who, being instructed in his will, hastens whither God calls him. Where can we learn his will, but in his word? Therefore in our actions we ought to regard the will of God, which is declared in his word. God only requires of us conformity to his precepts. If we do any thing contrary to them, it is not obedience, but contumacy and transgression. But it is said, if he would not permit it, we should not do it. This I grant. But do we perform evil actions with the design of pleasing him? He gives us no such command. We precipitate ourselves into them, not considering what is his will, but inflamed with the violence of our passions, so that we deliberately strive to oppose him. In this manner even by criminal actions we subserve his righteous ordination; because, in the infinite greatness of his wisdom, he well knows how to use evil instruments for the accomplishment of good purposes. Now, observe the absurdity of their reasoning: they wish the authors of crimes to escape with impunity, because crimes are not perpetrated but by the ordination of God. I admit more than this; even that thieves, and homicides, and other malefactors, are instruments of Divine providence, whom the Lord uses for the execution of the judgments which he has appointed. But I deny that this ought to afford any excuse for their crimes. For will they either implicate God in the same iniquity with themselves, or cover their depravity with his righteousness? They can do neither. They are prevented from exculpating themselves, by the reproofs of their own consciences; and they can lay no blame upon God, for they find in themselves nothing but evil, and in him only a legitimate use of their wickedness. But it is alleged that he operates by their means. And whence, I ask, proceeds the fetid smell of a carcass, which has been putrefied and disclosed by the heat of the sun? It is visible to all that it is excited by the solar rays; yet no person on this account attributes to those rays an offensive smell. So, when the matter and guilt of evil resides in a bad man, why should God be supposed to contract any defilement, if he uses his service according to his own pleasure? Let us dismiss this petulance, therefore, which may rail against the justice of God from a distance, but can never reach that Divine attribute.

VI. But these cavils, or rather extravagancies of frenzy, will easily be dispelled by the pious and holy contemplation of providence, which the rule of piety dictates to us, so that we may derive from it the greatest pleasure and advantage. The mind of a Christian, therefore, when it is certainly persuaded that all things happen by the ordination of God, and that there is nothing fortuitously contingent, will always direct its views to him as the supreme cause of all things, and will also consider inferior causes in their proper order. He will not doubt that the particular providence of God is watchful for his preservation, never permitting any event which it will not overrule for his advantage and safety. But, since he is concerned in the first place with men, and in the next place with the other creatures, he will assure himself, as to both, that the providence of God reigns over all. With respect to men, whether good or evil, he will acknowledge that their deliberations, wills, endeavours, and powers, are under his control, so that it is at his option to direct them whithersoever he pleases, and to restrain them as often as he pleases. The vigilance of the particular providence of God for the safety of the faithful is attested by numerous and very remarkable promises: "Cast thy burden upon the Lord, and he shall sustain thee: he shall never suffer the righteous to be moved. He that dwelleth in the secret place of the Most High shall abide under the shadow of the Almighty. He that toucheth you, toucheth the apple of his eye. We have a strong city: salvation will God appoint for walls and bulwarks.

Though a woman forget her sucking child, yet will I not forget thee." Moreover, this is the principal scope of the Biblical histories, to teach us that the Lord so sedulously defends the ways of the saints, that they may not even "dash their foot against a stone." Therefore, as we have a little before justly exploded the opinion of those who hold a universal providence of God, which descends not to the care of every creature in particular, so it is principally necessary and useful to contemplate this special care towards ourselves. For this reason, Christ, after having asserted that not the meanest sparrow falls to the ground without the will of the Father, immediately makes the following application—that the more we exceed the value of sparrows, the greater care we should consider God as exercising over us; and he carries this to such an extent, that we may be confident that the hairs of our head are numbered. What more can we desire for ourselves, if not a single hair can fall from our head, but according to his will? I speak not exclusively of the human race; but since God has chosen the Church for his habitation, there is no doubt but he particularly displays his paternal care in the government of it.

VII. The servant of God, encouraged by these promises and examples, will add the testimonies, which inform us that all men are subject to his power, either to conciliate their minds in our favour, or to restrain their malice from being injurious. For it is the Lord who gives us favour, not only with our friends, but also in the eyes of the Egyptians; and he knows how to subdue, by various methods, the fury of our enemies. Sometimes he deprives them of understanding, so that they can form no sober or prudent plans; as he sent Satan to fill the mouths of all the prophets with falsehood, in order to deceive Ahab: he infatuated Rehoboam by the counsel of the young men, that through his own folly he might be spoiled of his kingdom. Sometimes, when he grants them understanding, he so terrifies and dispirits them, that they can neither determine nor undertake what they have conceived. Sometimes, also, when he has permitted them to attempt what their rage and passion prompted, he opportunely breaks their impetuosity, not suffering them to proceed to the accomplishment of their designs. Thus he prematurely defeated the counsel of Ahithophel, which would have been fatal to David. Thus, also, he takes care to govern all creatures for the benefit and safety of his people, even the devil himself, who, we see, dared not to attempt any thing against Job, without his permission and command. The necessary consequences of this knowledge are, gratitude in prosperity, patience in adversity, and a wonderful security respecting the future. Every prosperous and pleasing event, therefore, the pious man will ascribe entirely to God, whether his beneficence be received through the ministry of men, or by the assistance of inanimate creatures. For this will be the reflection of his mind: "It is certainly the Lord that has inclined their hearts to favour me, that has united them to me to be the instruments of his benignity towards me." In an abundance of the fruits of the earth, he will consider, that it is the Lord who regards the heaven, that the heaven may regard the earth, that the earth, also, may regard its own productions: in other things he will not doubt that it is the Divine benediction alone which is the cause of all prosperity; nor will he bear to be ungrateful after so many admonitions.

VIII. If any adversity befall him, in this case, also, he will immediately lift up his heart to God, whose hand is most capable of impressing us with patience and placid moderation of mind. If Joseph had dwelt on a review of the perfidy of his brethren, he never could have recovered his fraternal affection for them. But as he turned his mind to the Lord, he forgot their injuries, and was so inclined to mildness and clemency, as even voluntarily to administer consolation to them, saying, "It was not you that sent me hither, but God did send me before you to save your lives. Ye thought evil against me; but God meant it unto good." If Job had regarded the Chaldeans, by whom he was molested, he had been inflamed to revenge; but recognizing the event at the same time as the work of the Lord, he consoled himself with this very beautiful observation: "The Lord gave, and the Lord hath taken away; blessed be the name of the Lord." Thus David, when assailed by Shimei with reproachful language and with stones, if he had confined his views to man, would have animated his soldiers to retaliate the injury; but understanding that it was not done without the instigation of the Lord, he rather appeases them: "Let him curse," says he, "because the Lord hath said unto him, Curse David." In another place he imposes the same restraint on the intemperance of his grief: "I was dumb," says he, "I opened not my mouth; because thou didst it." If there be no more efficacious remedy for anger and impatience, surely that man has made no small proficiency, who has learned in this case to meditate on the Divine providence, that he may be able at all times to recall his mind to this consideration: "It is the will of the Lord, therefore it must be endured; not only because resistance is unlawful and vain, but because he wills nothing but what is both just and expedient." The conclusion of the whole is this—that, when we suffer injuries from men, forgetting their malice, which would only exasperate our grief and instigate our minds to revenge, we should remember to ascend to God, and learn to account it a certain truth, that whatever our enemies have criminally committed against us, has been permitted and directed by his righteous dispensation. To restrain us from retaliating injuries, Paul prudently admonishes us that our contention is not with flesh and blood, but with a spiritual enemy, the devil, in order that we may prepare ourselves for the contest. But this admonition is the most useful in appeasing all the sallies of resentment, that God arms for the conflict both the devil and all wicked men, and sits himself as the arbiter of the combat, to exercise our patience. But if the calamities and miseries which oppress us happen without the interposition of men, let us recollect the doctrine of the law, that every prosperous event proceeds from the benediction of God, but that all adverse ones are his maledictions; and let us tremble at that awful denunciation, "If ye will walk contrary unto me, then will I also walk contrary unto you;" language which reproves our stupidity, while, according to the common apprehensions of the flesh, esteeming every event, both prosperous and adverse, to be fortuitous, we are neither animated to the worship of God by his benefits, nor stimulated to repentance by his corrections. This is the reason of the sharp expostulations of Jeremiah and of Amos, because the Jews supposed that both good and evil events came to pass without any appointment of God. To the same purpose is this passage of Isaiah: "I form the light, and create darkness: I make peace, and create evil: I the Lord do all these things."

IX. Yet at the same time a pious man will not overlook inferior causes. Nor, because he accounts those from whom he has received any benefit, the ministers of the Divine goodness, will he therefore pass them by unnoticed, as though they deserved no thanks for their kindness; but will feel, and readily acknowledge, his obligation to them, and study to return it as ability and opportunity may permit. Finally, he will reverence and praise God as the principal Author of benefits received, but will honour men as his ministers; and will understand, what, indeed, is the fact, that the will of God has laid him under obligations to those persons by whose means the Lord has been pleased to communicate his benefits. If he suffer any loss either through negligence or through imprudence, he will conclude that it happened according to the Divine will, but will also impute the blame of it to himself. If any one be removed by disease, whom, while it was his duty to take care of him, he has treated with neglect,—though he cannot be ignorant that that person had reached those limits which it was impossible for him to pass, yet he will not make this a plea to extenuate his guilt; but, because he has not faithfully performed his duty towards him, will consider him as having perished through his criminal negligence. Much less, when fraud and preconceived malice appear in the perpetration either of murder or of theft, will he excuse those enormities under the pretext of the Divine providence: in the same crime he will distinctly contemplate the righteousness of God and the iniquity of man, as they respectively discover themselves. But it is principally in regard to things future that he will direct his attention to inferior causes of this kind. For he will rank it among the blessings of the Lord, not to be destitute of human aids which he may use for his own safety; he will neither be remiss, therefore, in taking the advice, nor negligent in imploring the help, of those whom he perceives to be capable of affording him assistance; but, considering all the creatures, that can in any respect be serviceable to him, as so many gifts from the Lord, he will use them as the legitimate instruments of the Divine providence. And as he is uncertain respecting the issue of his undertakings, except that he knows that the Lord will in all things provide for his good, he studiously aims at what, according to the best judgment he can form, will be for his advantage. Nor, in conducting his deliberations, will he be carried away by his own opinion, but will recommend and resign himself to the wisdom of God, that he may be directed by its guidance to the right end. But he will not place his confidence in external helps to such a degree as, if possessed of them, securely to rely on them, or, if destitute of them, to tremble with despair. For his mind will always be fixed solely on the Divine providence, nor will he suffer himself to be seduced from a steady contemplation of it, by any consideration of present things. Thus Joab, though he acknowledges the event of battle to depend on the will and the power of God, yet surrenders not himself to inactivity, but sedulously executes all the duties of his office, and leaves the event to the Divine decision. "Let us play the men," says he, "for our people, and for the cities of our God; and the Lord do that which seemeth him good." This knowledge will divest us of temerity and false confidence, and excite us to continual invocations of God; it will also support our minds with a good hope, that without hesitation we may securely and magnanimously despise all the dangers which surround us.

X. Herein is discovered the inestimable felicity of the pious mind. Human life is beset by innumerable evils, and threatened with a thousand deaths. Not to go beyond ourselves,—since our body is the receptacle of a thousand diseases, and even contains and fosters the causes of diseases, a man must unavoidably carry about with him destruction in unnumbered forms, and protract a life which is, as it were, involved in death. For what else can you say of it, when neither cold nor heat in any considerable degree can be endured without danger? Now, whithersoever you turn, all the objects around you are not only unworthy of your confidence, but almost openly menace you, and seem to threaten immediate death. Embark in a ship; there is but a single step between you and death. Mount a horse; the slipping of one foot endangers your life. Walk through the streets of a city; you are liable to as many dangers as there are tiles on the roofs. If there be a sharp weapon in your hand, or that of your friend, the mischief is manifest. All the ferocious animals you see are armed for your destruction. If you endeavour to shut yourself in a garden surrounded with a good fence, and exhibiting nothing but what is delightful, even there sometimes lurks a serpent. Your house, perpetually liable to fire, menaces you by day with poverty, and by night with falling on your head. Your land, exposed to hail, frost, drought, and various tempests, threatens you with sterility, and with its attendant, famine. I omit poison, treachery, robbery, and open violence, which partly beset us at home, and partly pursue us abroad. Amidst these difficulties, must not man be most miserable, who is half dead while he lives, and is dispirited and alarmed as though he had a sword perpetually applied to his neck? You will say that these things happen seldom, or certainly not always, nor to every man, but never all at once. I grant it; but as we are admonished by the examples of others, that it is possible for them to happen also to us, and that we have no more claim to exemption from them than others, we must unavoidably dread them as events that we may expect. What can you imagine more calamitous than such a dread? Besides, it is an insult to God to say that he has exposed man, the noblest of his creatures, to the blindness and temerity of fortune. But here I intend to speak only of the misery which man must feel, if he be subject to the dominion of fortune.

XI. On the contrary, when this light of Divine providence has once shined on a pious man, he is relieved and delivered not only from the extreme anxiety and dread with which he was previously oppressed, but also from all care. For, as he justly dreads fortune, so he ventures securely to commit himself to God. This, I say, is his consolation, to apprehend that his heavenly Father restrains all things by his power, governs all things by his will, and regulates all things by his wisdom, in such a manner, that nothing can happen but by his appointment; moreover, that God has taken him under his protection, and committed him to the care of angels, so that he can sustain no injury from water, or fire, or sword, any further than the Divine Governor may be pleased to permit. For thus sings the Psalmist: "Surely he shall deliver thee from the snare of the fowler, and from the noisome pestilence. He shall cover thee with his feathers, and under his wings shalt thou trust: his truth shall be thy shield and buckler. Thou shalt not be afraid for the terror by night; nor for the arrow that flieth by day; nor for the pestilence that walketh in darkness; nor for the destruction that wasteth at noonday." Hence also proceeds that confidence of glorying in the saints: "The Lord is on my side; I will not fear what man can do unto me. The Lord is the strength of my life; of whom shall I be afraid? Though a host should encamp against me—though I walk through the valley of the shadow of death, I will fear no evil." How is it that their security remains unshaken, while the world appears to be revolving at random, but because they know that the Lord is universally operative, and confide in his operations as beneficial to them? Now, when their safety is attacked, either by the devil or by wicked men, if they were not supported by the recollection and contemplation of providence, they must necessarily and immediately faint. But when they recollect, that the devil and the whole army of the wicked are in every respect so restrained by the Divine power, that they can neither conceive of any hostility against us, nor, after having conceived it, form a plan for its accomplishment, nor even move a finger towards the execution of such plan, any further than he has permitted, and even commanded them; and that they are not only bound by his chains, but also compelled to do him service,—they have an abundant source of consolation. For as it belongs to the Lord to arm their fury, and to direct it to whatever objects he pleases, so it also belongs to him to fix its limits, that they may not enjoy an unbounded triumph according to their own wills. Established in this persuasion, Paul determined his journey in one place by the permission of God, which in another he had declared was prevented by Satan. If he had only said that Satan was the obstacle, he would have appeared to attribute too much power to him, as though he were able to subvert the purposes of God; but when he states God to be the arbiter, on whose permission all journeys depend, he at the same time shows, that Satan, with all his machinations, can effect nothing but by his permission. For the same reason, David, on account of the various and constant vicissitudes of life, betakes himself to this asylum: "My times are in thy hand." He might have mentioned either the course of life, or *time*, in the singular number; but by the word *times* he intended to express, that, however unstable the condition of men may be, all the vicissitudes which take place are under the government of God. For which reason Rezin and the king of Israel, when, after the junction of their forces for the destruction of Judah, they resembled firebrands kindled to consume and ruin the land, are called by the Prophet "smoking firebrands," which can do nothing but emit a little smoke. Thus Pharaoh, when his riches, his strength, and the multitude of his forces, rendered him formidable to all, is himself compared to a sea-monster, and his forces to fishes. Therefore God denounces that he will take both the captain and his army with his hook, and draw them whither he pleases. Finally, to dwell no longer on this part of the subject, you will easily perceive, on examination, that ignorance of providence is the greatest of miseries, but that the knowledge of it is attended with the highest felicity.

XII. On the doctrine of Divine providence, as far as it may conduce to the solid instruction and consolation of the faithful, (for to satisfy a vain curiosity is neither possible nor desirable,) enough would now have been said, were it not for a difficulty arising from a few passages, which apparently imply, in opposition to what has been stated, that the counsel of God is not firm and stable, but liable to change according to the situation of sublunary affairs. In the first place, there are several instances in which repentance is attributed to God; as, that he repented of having created man, and of having exalted Saul to the kingdom; and that he will repent of the evil which he had determined to inflict on his people, as soon as he shall have perceived their conversion. In the next place, we read of the abrogation of some of his decrees. By Jonah he declared to the Ninevites, that, after the lapse of forty days, Nineveh should be destroyed; but their penitence afterwards obtained from him a more merciful sentence. By the mouth of Isaiah he denounced death to Hezekiah; which the prayers and tears of that monarch moved him to defer. Hence many persons argue, that God has not fixed the affairs of men by an eternal decree; but that every year, day, and hour, he decrees one thing or another, according to the respective merits of each individual, or to his own ideas of equity and justice. With regard to repentance, we must not admit that it can happen to God, any more than ignorance, or error, or impotence. For if no man knowingly and willingly lays himself under the necessity of repentance, we cannot attribute repentance to God, without saying either that he is ignorant of the future, or that he cannot avoid it, or that he precipitately and inconsiderately adopts a resolution, of which he immediately repents. But that is so far from the meaning of the Holy Spirit, that in the very mention of repentance, he denies that it can belong to God, because "he is not a man, that he should repent." And it must be remarked, that both these points are so connected in the same chapter, that a comparison fully reconciles the apparent inconsistency. Where it is said that God repented of having created Saul king, the change declared to have taken place is figurative. It is almost immediately added, that "The strength of Israel will not lie nor repent; for he is not a man, that he should repent;" in which, without any figure, his immutability is plainly asserted. It is certain, therefore, that the ordination of God in the administration of human affairs, is perpetual, and superior to all repentance. And to place his constancy beyond all doubt, even his adversaries have been constrained to attest it. For Balaam, notwithstanding his reluctance, was obliged to break out into the following exclamation: "God is not a man, that he should lie; neither the son of man, that he should repent: hath he said, and shall he not do it? or hath he spoken, and shall he not make it good?"

XIII. How, then, it will be inquired, is the term *repentance* to be understood, when attributed to God? I reply, in the same manner as all the other forms of expression, which describe God to us after the manner of men. For, since our infirmity cannot reach his sublimity, the description of him which is given to us, in order that we may understand it, must be lowered to the level of our capacity. His method of lowering it, is to represent himself to us, not as he is in himself, but according to our perception of him. Though he is free from all perturbation of mind, he declares that he is angry with sinners. As, therefore, when we hear that God is angry, we ought not to imagine any commotion in him, but rather to consider this expression as borrowed from our perception, because God carries the appearance of one who is very angry, whenever he executes judgment,—so neither by the term *repentance* ought we to understand any thing but a change of actions; because men are accustomed to express their dissatisfaction with themselves by changing their actions. Since every change among men, therefore, is a correction of that which displeases them, and correction proceeds from repentance, therefore the term *repentance* is used to signify that God makes a change in his works. Yet, at the same time, there is no alteration in his counsel or his will, nor any change in his affections; but how sudden soever the variation may appear to the eyes of men, he perpetually and regularly prosecutes what he has foreseen, approved, and decreed from eternity.

XIV. Nor does the Sacred History, when it records the remission of the destruction which had just been denounced against the Ninevites, and the prolongation of the life of Hezekiah after he had been threatened with death, prove that there was any abrogation of the Divine decrees. Persons who thus understand it, are deceived in their ideas of the threatenings; which, though expressed in the form of simple declarations, yet, as the event shows, contain in them a tacit condition. For why did God send Jonah to the Ninevites, to predict the ruin of their city? Why did he, by the mouth of Isaiah, warn Hezekiah of death? He could have destroyed both them and him, without previously announcing their end. He had some other object in view, therefore, than to forewarn them of their death, and to give them a distant prospect of its approach. And that was not to destroy them, but to reform them, that they might not be destroyed. Therefore the prediction of Jonah, that after forty days Nineveh should fall, was uttered to prevent its fall. Hezekiah was deprived of the hope of a longer life, in order that he might obtain a prolongation of it in answer to his prayers. Now, who does not see, that the Lord, by such denunciations as these, intended to arouse to repentance the persons whom he thus alarmed, that they might escape the judgment which their sins had deserved? If this be admitted, the nature of the circumstances leads to the conclusion, that we must understand a tacit condition implied in the simple denunciation. This is also confirmed by similar examples. The Lord, reprehending king Abimelech for having deprived Abraham of his wife, uses these words:—"Behold, thou art but a dead man, for the woman which thou hast taken; for she is a man's wife." But after Abimelech has excused himself, the Lord speaks in this manner: "Restore the man his wife; for he is a prophet, and he shall pray for thee, and thou shalt live; and if thou restore her not, know thou that thou shalt surely die, thou, and all that are thine." You see how, by the first declaration, God terrifies his mind, to dispose him to make satisfaction; but in the next, he makes an explicit declaration of his will. Since other passages are to be explained in a similar manner, you must not infer that there is any abrogation of a prior purpose of the Lord, because he may have annulled some former declarations. For God rather prepares the way for his eternal ordination, when, by a denunciation of punishment, he calls to repentance those whom he designs to spare, than makes any variation in his will, or even in his declarations, except that he does not syllabically express what, nevertheless, is easily understood. For that assertion of Isaiah must remain true: "The Lord of hosts hath purposed, and who shall disannul it? and his hand is stretched out, and who shall turn it back?"

7.

God Uses the Agency of the Impious, And Inclines Their Minds to Execute His Judgments, Yet Without the Least Stain of His Perfect Purity.

A question of greater difficulty arises from other passages, where God is said to incline or draw, according to his own pleasure, Satan himself and all the reprobate. For the carnal understanding scarcely comprehends how he, acting by their means, contracts no defilement from their criminality, and, even in operations common to himself and them, is free from every fault, and yet righteously condemns those whose ministry he uses. Hence was invented the distinction between *doing* and *permitting*; because to many persons this has appeared an inexplicable difficulty, that Satan and all the impious are subject to the power and government of God, so that he directs their malice to whatever end he pleases, and uses their crimes for the execution of his judgments. The modesty of those who are alarmed at the appearance of absurdity, might perhaps be excusable, if they did not attempt to vindicate the Divine justice from all accusation by a pretence utterly destitute of any foundation in truth. They consider it absurd that a man should be blinded by the will and command of God, and afterwards be punished for his blindness. They therefore evade the difficulty, by alleging that it happens only by the permission, and not by the will of God; but God himself, by the most unequivocal declarations, rejects this subterfuge. That men, however, can effect nothing but by the secret will of God, and can deliberate on nothing but what he has previously decreed, and determines by his secret direction, is proved by express and innumerable testimonies. What we have before cited from the Psalmist, that "God hath done whatsoever he hath pleased," undoubtedly pertains to all the actions of men. If God be the certain arbiter of war and peace, as is there affirmed, and that without any exception, who will venture to assert, that he remains ignorant and unconcerned respecting men, while they are actuated by the blind influence of chance? But this subject will be better elucidated by particular examples. From the first chapter of Job we know that Satan presents himself before God to receive his commands, as well as the angels, who yield a spontaneous obedience. It is, indeed, in a different manner, and for a different end; yet he cannot attempt any thing but by the Divine will. Although he seems to obtain only a bare permission to afflict that holy man, yet, since this sentence is true, "The Lord gave, and the Lord hath taken away," we conclude that God was the author of that trial, of which Satan and mischievous robbers and assassins were the immediate agents. Satan endeavours to drive him by desperation into madness. The Sabeans, in a predatory incursion, cruelly and wickedly seize upon property not their own. Job acknowledges that he was stripped of all his wealth, and reduced to poverty, because such was the will of God. Therefore, whatever is attempted by men, or by Satan himself, God still holds the helm, to direct all their attempts to the execution of his judgments. God intends the deception of that perfidious king Ahab; the devil offers his service for that purpose; he is sent with a positive commission to be a lying spirit in the mouth of all the prophets. If the blinding and infatuation of Ahab be a Divine judgment, the pretence of bare permission disappears. For it would be ridiculous for a judge merely to permit, without decreeing what should be done, and commanding his officers to execute it. The Jews designed to destroy Christ; Pilate and his soldiers complied with their outrageous violence; yet the disciples, in a solemn prayer, confess that all the impious did nothing but what "the hand and the counsel of God determined before to be done;" agreeably to what Peter had already preached, that he was "delivered by the determinate counsel and foreknowledge of God," that he might be "crucified and slain." As though he had said that God, who saw every thing from the beginning, with a clear knowledge and determined will, appointed what the Jews executed; as he mentions in another place: "Those things which God before had showed by the mouth of all his prophets, that Christ should suffer, he hath so fulfilled." Absalom, defiling his father's bed with incest, perpetrated a detestable crime; yet God pronounces that this was his work; for his words are, "Thou didst it secretly; but I will do this thing before all Israel, and before the sun." Whatever cruelty the Chaldeans exercised in Judea, Jeremiah pronounces to be the work of God; for which reason Nebuchadnezzar is called the servant of God. God frequently proclaims, that the impious are excited to war by his hissing, by the sound of his trumpet, by his influence, and by his command: he calls the Assyrian the rod of his anger, and the staff which he moves with his hand. The destruction of the holy city and the ruin of the temple he calls his own work. David, not murmuring against God, but acknowledging him to be a righteous Judge, confesses the maledictions of Shimei to proceed from his command. "The Lord," says he, "hath said unto him, Curse." It often occurs in the Sacred History, that whatever comes to pass proceeds from the Lord; as the defection of the ten tribes, the death of the sons of Eli, and many events of a similar kind. Those who are but moderately acquainted with the Scriptures will perceive that, for the sake of brevity, out of a great number of testimonies, I have produced only a few; which, nevertheless, abundantly evince how nugatory and insipid it is, instead of the providence of God, to substitute a bare permission; as though God were sitting in a watchtower, expecting fortuitous events, and so his decisions were dependent on the will of men.

II. With respect to his secret influences, the declaration of Solomon concerning the heart of a king, that it is inclined hither or thither according to the Divine will, certainly extends to the whole human race, and is as much as though he had said, that whatever conceptions we form in our minds, they are directed by the secret inspiration of God. And certainly, if he did not operate internally on the human mind, there would be no propriety in asserting, that he causes "the wisdom of the wise to perish, and the understanding of the prudent to be hid; that he poureth contempt upon princes, and causeth them to wander in the wilderness, where there is no way." And to this alludes, what we frequently read, that men are timorous, as their hearts are possessed with his fear. Thus David departed from the camp of Saul, without the knowledge of any one; "because a deep sleep from the Lord was fallen upon them all." But nothing can be desired more explicit than his frequent declarations, that he blinds the minds of men, strikes them with giddiness, inebriates them with the spirit of slumber, fills them with infatuation, and hardens their hearts. These passages also many persons refer to permission, as though, in abandoning the reprobate, God permitted them to be blinded by Satan. But that solution is too frivolous, since the Holy Spirit expressly declares that their blindness and infatuation are inflicted by the righteous judgment of God. He is said to have caused the obduracy of Pharaoh's heart, and also to have aggravated and confirmed it. Some elude the force of these expressions with a foolish cavil—that, since Pharaoh himself is elsewhere said to have hardened his own heart, his own will is stated as the cause of his obduracy; as though these two things were at all incompatible with each other, that man should be actuated by God, and yet at the same time be active himself. But I retort on them their own objection; for if *hardening* denotes a bare permission, Pharaoh cannot properly be charged with being the cause of his own obstinacy. Now, how weak and insipid would be such an interpretation, as though Pharaoh only permitted himself to be hardened! Besides, the Scripture cuts off all occasion for such cavils. God says, "I will harden his heart." So, also, Moses says, concerning the inhabitants of Canaan, that they marched forth to battle, because the Lord had hardened their hearts; which is likewise repeated by another Prophet— "He turned their hearts to hate his people." Thus, also, in Isaiah, he declares he will "send the Assyrian against a hypocritical nation, and will give him a charge to take the spoil, and to take the prey;" not that he meant to teach impious and refractory men a voluntary obedience, but because he would incline them to execute his judgments, just as if they had his commands engraven on their minds. Hence it appears that they were impelled by the positive appointment of God. I grant, indeed, that God often actuates the reprobate by the interposition of Satan; but in such a manner that Satan himself acts his part by the Divine impulse, and proceeds to the extent of the Divine appointment. Saul was disturbed by an evil spirit; but it is said to be "from the Lord;" to teach us that Saul's madness proceeded from the righteous vengeance of God. Satan is also said to blind "the minds of them which believe not;" but the strength of the delusion proceeds from God himself, "that they should believe a lie, who believe not the truth." According to one view of the subject, it is said, "If the prophet be deceived when he hath spoken a thing, I the Lord have deceived that prophet." But, according to another, God is said himself to "give men over to a reprobate mind," and to the vilest lusts; because he is the principal author of his own righteous vengeance, and Satan is only the dispenser of it. But as we must discuss this subject again in the second book, where we shall treat of the freedom or slavery of the human will, I think I have now said, in a brief manner, as much as the occasion required. The whole may be summed up thus; that, as the will of God is said to be the cause of all things, his providence is established as the governor in all the counsels and works of men, so that it not only exerts its power in the elect, who are influenced by the Holy Spirit, but also compels the compliance of the reprobate.

III. But, as I have hitherto only recited such things as are delivered without any obscurity or ambiguity in the Scriptures, let persons who hesitate not to brand with ignominy those oracles of heaven, beware what kind of opposition they make. For, if they pretend ignorance, with a desire to be commended for their modesty, what greater instance of pride can be conceived, than to oppose one little word to the authority of God! as, "It appears otherwise to me," or, "I would rather not meddle with this subject." But if they openly censure, what will they gain by their puny attempts against heaven? Their petulance, indeed, is no novelty; for in all ages there have been impious and profane men, who have virulently opposed this doctrine. But they shall feel the truth of what the Spirit long ago declared by the mouth of David, that God "is clear when he judgeth." David obliquely hints at the madness of men who display such excessive presumption amidst their insignificance, as not only to dispute against God, but to arrogate to themselves the power of condemning him. In the mean time, he briefly suggests, that God is unaffected by all the blasphemies which they discharge against heaven, but that he dissipates the mists of calumny, and illustriously displays his righteousness; our faith, also, being founded on the Divine word, and therefore, superior to all the world, from its exaltation looks down with contempt upon those mists. For their first objection, that, if nothing happens but by the will of God, he has in him two contrary wills, because he decrees in his secret counsel what he has publicly prohibited in his law, is easily refuted. But before I reply, I wish the reader again to be apprized, that this cavil is directed, not against me, but against the Holy Spirit, who dictated to the pious Job this confession, that what had befallen him had happened according to the Divine will: when he had been plundered by banditti, he acknowledged in their injuries the righteous scourge of God. What says the Scripture in another case? "They," the sons of Eli, "hearkened not unto the voice of their father, because the Lord would slay them." The Psalmist also exclaims, that "God," who "is in the heavens, hath done whatsoever he hath pleased." And now I have sufficiently proved, that God is called the author of all those things, which, according to the system of these censors, happen only by his uninfluential permission. He declares that he creates light and darkness, that he forms good and evil, and that no evil occurs, which he has not performed. Let them say, then, whether he exercises his judgments voluntarily or involuntarily. But as Moses suggests, that he who is killed by the fortuitous fall of an axe, is delivered by God to the stroke, so in the Acts, the whole church asserts that Herod and Pilate conspired to do what the hand and the counsel of God had predetermined. And indeed, unless the crucifixion of Christ was according to the will of God, what becomes of our redemption? Yet the will of God is neither repugnant to itself, nor subject to change, nor chargeable with pretending to dislike what it approves; but whilst in him it is uniform and simple, it wears to us the appearance of variety; because the weakness of our understanding comprehends not how the same thing may be in different respects both agreeable to his will, and contrary to it. Paul, after having said that the vocation of the Gentiles was a hidden mystery, adds, that it contained a manifestation of the manifold wisdom of God. Now, because, through the dulness of our capacity, the Divine wisdom appears to us manifold, (or multiform, as it has been translated by an ancient interpreter,) shall we therefore dream of any vanity in God himself, as though his counsels were mutable, or his thoughts contradictory to each other? Rather, while we comprehend not how God intends that to be done, the doing of which he forbids, let us remember our imbecility, and at the same time consider, that the light which he inhabits, is justly called inaccessible, because it is overspread with impenetrable darkness. Therefore all pious and modest men will easily acquiesce in this opinion of Augustine: "That a man may sometimes choose, with a good intention, that which is not agreeable to the will of God; as, if a good son wishes his father to live, whilst God determines that he shall die. It is also possible for a man to will with a bad design, what God wills with a good one; as, if a bad son wishes his father to die, which is also the will of God. Now, the former wishes what is not agreeable, the latter what is agreeable to the Divine will. And yet the filial affection of the former is more consonant to the righteous will of God, than the want of natural affection in the latter, though it accords with his secret design. So great is the difference between what belongs to the human will, and what to the Divine, and between the ends to which the will of every one is to be referred, for approbation or censure. For God fulfils his righteous will by the wicked wills of wicked men." This writer had just before said, that the apostate angels, and all the reprobate, in their defection, acted, as far as respected themselves, in direct opposition to the Divine will; but that this was not possible with respect to the Divine omnipotence; because, while they are opposing the will of God, his will is accomplished concerning them. Whence he exclaims, "The works of the Lord are great, prepared according to all his determinations;" so that, in a wonderful and ineffable manner, that is not done without his will which yet is contrary to his will; because it would not be done if he did not permit it; and this permission is not involuntary, but voluntary; nor would his goodness permit the perpetration of any evil, unless his omnipotence were able even from that evil to educe good.

IV. In the same manner we answer, or rather annihilate, another objection—that, if God not only uses the agency of the impious, but governs their designs and affections, he is the author of all crimes; and therefore men are undeservedly condemned, if they execute what God has decreed, because they obey his will. For his will is improperly confounded with his precept, between which innumerable examples evince the difference to be very great. For although, when Absalom defiled the wives of his father, it was the will of God by this disgrace to punish the adultery of David, he did not therefore command that abandoned son to commit incest, unless perhaps with respect to David, as he speaks of the reproaches of Shimei. For when he confesses Shimei's maledictions to proceed from the Divine command, he by no means commends his obedience, as though that impudent and worthless man were fulfilling a Divine precept; but acknowledging his tongue as the scourge of God, he patiently submits to the chastisement. Let it be remembered, that whilst God by means of the impious fulfils his secret decrees, they are not excusable, as though they were obedient to his precepts, which they wantonly and intentionally violate. The direction of the perverse actions of men, by the secret providence of God, is illustriously exemplified in the election of Jeroboam to the regal dignity. The temerity and infatuation of the people in this proceeding are severely condemned, because they perverted the order established by God, and perfidiously revolted from the family of David; and yet we know that this event was agreeable to the Divine will. Whence there is an appearance of contradiction also in the language of Hosea; for in one place God complains that the erection of that kingdom was without his knowledge and against his will; but in another declares that he gave Jeroboam to be a king in his anger. How can these things be reconciled, that Jeroboam did not reign by the will of God, and yet that God appointed him to be king? Why, thus: because neither could the people revolt from the family of David, without shaking off the yoke which God had imposed upon them; nor yet was God deprived of the liberty of thus punishing the ingratitude of Solomon. We see, then, how God, while he hates perfidy, yet righteously and with a different design decrees the defection; whence also Jeroboam is, beyond all expectation, constrained by the holy unction to assume the regal office. In the same manner, the Sacred History relates, that God raised up an enemy, to deprive the son of Solomon of part of the kingdom. Let the reader diligently consider both these things: because it had pleased God that the people should be under the government of one king, their division into two parts was contrary to his will; and yet from his will the schism first originated. For certainly since a Prophet, both by a prediction and by the ceremony of unction, excited a hope of succeeding to the kingdom, in the mind of Jeroboam, who before entertained not a thought of such an event, this could not be done, either without the knowledge, or against the will, of God, who commanded it to be done; and yet the rebellion of the people is justly condemned, because, in opposition to the Divine will, they revolted from the posterity of David. Thus, also, it is afterwards subjoined, that "the cause" of the haughty contempt of the people manifested by Rehoboam "was of God, that the Lord might perform his word, which he spake by the hand of Ahijah" his servant. See how the sacred union is divided, in opposition to the will of God, and yet by his will the ten tribes are alienated from the son of Solomon. Let us add another similar example, where, with the consent, and even by the assistance of the people, the sons of Ahab are massacred, and all his posterity exterminated. Jehu, indeed, truly observed that "there had fallen unto the earth nothing of the word of the Lord," but that he had "done that which he spake by his servant Elijah." And yet he justly reprehends the citizens of Samaria for having lent their assistance. "Are ye righteous?" says he; "behold, I conspired against my master, and slew him; but who slew all these?" If I am not deceived, I have now clearly explained how the same act displays the criminality of men and the justice of God. And to modest minds this answer of Augustine will always be sufficient: "Since God delivered Christ, and Christ delivered his own body, and Judas delivered the Lord, why, in this delivery, is God righteous and man guilty? Because in the same act, they acted not from the same cause." But if any persons find greater difficulty in what we now assert, that there is no consent between God and man, in cases where man by his righteous influence commits unlawful actions, let them remember what is advanced by Augustine in another place: "Who can but tremble at those judgments, when God does even in the hearts of the wicked whatsoever he pleases, and yet renders to them according to their demerits?" And certainly it would no more be right to attribute to God the blame of the perfidy of Judas, because he decreed the delivery of his Son, and actually delivered him to death, than to transfer to Judas the praise of redemption. Therefore the same writer elsewhere informs us, that in this scrutiny God inquires, not what men could have done, nor what they have done, but what they intended to do, that he may take cognizance of their design and their will. Let those to whom there appears any harshness in this procedure, consider a little how far their obstinacy is tolerable, while they reject a truth which is attested by plain testimonies of Scripture, because it exceeds their comprehension, and condemn the publication of those things which God, unless he had known that the knowledge of them would be useful, would never have commanded to be taught by his Prophets and Apostles. For our wisdom ought to consist in embracing with gentle docility, and without any exception, all that is delivered in the sacred Scriptures. But those who oppose this doctrine with less modesty and greater violence, since it is evident that their opposition is against God, are unworthy of a longer refutation.

Note

If you wish to read more of this text, you can find it in Calvin's *Institutes of the Christian Religion*, Book I.

Enjoyed your Christian reading?

Don't end your introduction to Christian literature here.

Send a blank email to

thegoodchristian10@gmail.com

for access to Christian audiobooks.

9 789360 072087